Laying it on the Line with God

The Risk of Honest Prayer

Charlie Walton

HillCrest
PUBLISHING

Laying it on the Line with God: The Risk of Honest Prayer

HillCrest
PUBLISHING

1648 Campus Court
Abilene, TX 79601
www.hillcrestpublishing.com

Cover design and typesetting by Tigris Creative Studios, LLC, Fort Worth, Texas.
www.tigrisstudios.com

Printed in the United States of America

ISBN 0-89112-437-3

Library of Congress Card Number 00-100806

2,3,4,5

**Dedicated to
John and Virginia Walton**
who taught me the power of the right word and the
power of persistent prayer.

Thanks also for stories and examples shared by
Glenn Owen, Jerry Porter, Marilyn Sharbach,
Jackie Steele, Mark Whitworth, and John Yackel.

Table
of Contents

1   The Emperor's Clothes..7
2   Prayer? Nothing To It..13
3   All I Really Want Is Everything............................19
4   What's the Deal Here, God? 25
5   "Plunk Your Magic Twanger, Froggy!"...................31
6   Thou Shalt Not Pray! 37
7   What If I Pray Wrong? 43
8   Even Asking for the Bad Stuff! 51
9   What We Have Here is a Failure to Communicate.......57
10 Remembering You Always in My Prayers...................67
11 The Ultimate E-Mail 77
12 Might As Well Lay It On the Line 87
13 Shut Up and Listen! 95
14 Does God Speak Olde English? 99
15 Do I Get Extra Points for Praying on Mountaintops? 105
16 Do Kneelers Get Preferential Treatment? 111
17 Public Prayers and Public Pray-ers 119
18 Can I Substitute Prayer for Sweat? 127
19 Persistent Prayer or Browbeating God? 135
20 So, It All Comes Down To... 141
    Suggested Readings...147
    Discussion and Study Questions...............................149

Chapter 1
The Emperor's Clothes

I like writing. For years, I have earned a living putting things into words. No one has ever accused me of writing great literature, but a lot of people *have* said, "You know, none of us here really understood our operation until you explained it in that brochure you wrote for us." They may say "in that brochure," or "in that article," or "in that video script." But the point is that I've been pretty successful explaining things — sometimes really complicated things — to everyday folks.

I wish I could tell you that this talent for simplifying things was the result of superior intelligence. But the truth is a little more humbling than that. My success as an explainer results mainly from the fact that I have to boil things down into such simple terms for *me* to understand them that in the process I end up putting them into words that the average, non-reading, partially distracted, semi-disinterested reader or viewer can understand.

But that's enough about my good fortune at turning a weakness into an occupation. This writing project may be the one that teaches me not to brag on the first page of a book, because this book is about a complex topic that has been baffling humans for thousands of years. It's one of those subjects that is simultaneously simple and complex. At first mention, most folks think they understand it pretty well. But if you ask them a couple of questions that explore below those surface understandings, you end up with an answer something like, "Well, I don't claim to understand all that theological stuff. I just know I believe in it."

This book is about prayer. You would think a book on prayer might be the last thing people would be interested in since most surveys indicate that around three-fourths of the population claim to pray at least once a week and half of us claim to pray every day. And as many as a fifth of people who claim to be atheists or agnostics usually surprise polltakers by claiming to pray with some regularity.

Sounds like we've got this prayer thing figured out. And yet, there are over 2,000 current books in print on the subject and library shelves are full of lots more books on prayer. Most religious booksellers will tell you that, after the Bible itself, books on prayer are their best sellers. A preacher friend of mine tells me that anytime you put out a questionnaire to find out what people would like to study in Sunday School the subject of prayer is always going to come in among the top five suggestions.

Sounds like a subject on which additional books might not even be needed. And if that turns out to be the case, then I am writing this book just for me. That will still be worthwhile. In fact, I can't wait until it's finished so I can read it. I have a bunch of partial concepts and developing understandings about prayer that I'm looking forward to putting down on paper. I'll toss them all into the word processor, arrange and re-arrange for a while, then sort and edit a bit until I have an explanation of prayer that is simple enough for me to grasp. If I can reach that goal, it will have been a project worth doing. And maybe what helps me will end up clarifying a few helpful concepts for other folks too.

My basic dilemma about prayer is easy to state. For a while, I believe in it strongly and am fully confident that the Creator of the universe is listening with interest and concern to everything I have to say. Then, without warning my confidence fades and I start to wonder, "Who do I think I'm kidding! I no longer believe in the Tooth Fairy or the Easter Bunny and yet I'm still closing my eyes, bowing my head, and whispering my wants and wishes to the Creator of the universe."

That's when I start remembering the story of "The Emperor's New Clothes," a parable about the ridiculous lengths humans will travel to protect their pride. Already several hundred years old when Hans Christian Andersen put his spin on it, the story tells of an emperor who was so vain that he changed clothes several times a day and was always seeking the most beautiful clothing to wear. Two scoundrels decided to play on the emperor's vanity. They appeared before him claiming to be tailors who had invented a method of weaving cloth so light and fine that everyone would admire it — everyone except those who were *too stupid and incompetent to appreciate its quality.*

Neither the emperor nor any of his court was willing to admit to being stupid and incompetent and unable to see the invisible cloth. So, the emperor pranced around the throne room totally naked and all the members of his court complimented him on the beauty, the fit, the patterns, even the colors of his beautiful new suit. The emperor's loyal subjects heard about the wonderful suit of clothes and wanted a chance to admire it. So, a parade was organized. The emperor rode in a carriage wearing only his "birthday suit" and all his subjects praised the beauty of his marvelous new suit, rather than appear stupid or incompetent.

This insanity continued until the parade passed a small boy who was too young to fear what others thought. He responded quite plainly, "The emperor is naked!" The people around the boy rebuked him for being so stupid and incompetent, but the damage was done. Doubt had crept in. Even though the emperor proudly finished his parade, the people never again viewed the emperor's new clothes in quite the same way.

Most of the time, my faith in prayer is very positive. I am confident that God is there, listening like a loving Father, taking note of each and every item I mention. But occasionally — sometimes even in the middle of a prayer — I might stop cold and wonder, "What do I think I am doing? How much sense does it make for a grown man, an otherwise reasonable adult, to convince himself that he is sitting here in this little room having a heart-to-heart talk with the Chief Executive Officer of the universe? Really, Charlie! How logical is it that this prayer thing can actually be happening the way everyone says it does?"

Believing in prayer is pretty popular. Saints and sinners both take it for granted. Even the ungodly and the unchurched would rather not hear you question their ability to "get through to God" when they have an emergency. And if those people don't want anyone questioning prayer, it goes without saying that church people could come down pretty hard on you for wondering out loud whether the prayer thing really works. "Stupid" and "incompetent" would be mild next to the words they would use. In their rush to smooth the waves your questions have made, they might resort to words like "liberal" or "faithless" or even "heretic." They would most certainly question the *source* of your negative thoughts about prayer, a topic that ranks right up there with motherhood, the flag, and covered dish dinners.

I'm not sure about the source of my occasional doubts that my prayers are going beyond my own head. Church folks would probably be quick to tell me the devil is putting those doubts in my mind. And I suppose that if I were the devil I would see it as a pretty good investment of my time to go around whispering doubts into the ears of folks who are praying. On the other hand, when I'm having my doubts about prayer, I am usually pretty doubtful about the devil, too.

As a matter of fact, most anytime that I am having doubts about prayer, I am likely to be wondering about the whole religion thing: God and Jesus and God's Spirit... even covered dish dinners. I suppose that's the way it is with faith. Since it's all about something you can't see, your mind is either in or out: either believing the whole thing or doubting the whole thing. Oh, there is one other position besides believing and disbelieving. That position would occur when I am having some doubts but still acting like I am 100 percent confident. We could call that the "emperor's clothes" kind of faith. I think it happens a lot more than we want to admit. I know it happens a lot more with me than I admit.

So... for better or worse, I'm going to tell the truth as I work my way through this topic of prayer. Maybe it's a book just for me. Or, if you're reading along with me at this point, a publisher must have agreed that we all needed an honest look at prayer — needed to ask ourselves if this is the most phenomenal communication medium in the history of the universe, or just the emperor's new clothes.

Dear Father,

Once again, I'm rushing in where angels know better than to go. But my reasons are sincere, Lord. I'd really like to feel more confident about prayer. I've been hearing about it all my life — been working at it myself for a long time. Everybody says nice things about prayer but I don't think I see it really changing people's lives very often. Please lead me as I write, Father. Keep me out of the quagmires and help me to put down what I learn in a form that will lead people closer to You. Make it a book, Father, that points people to You. That is my purpose. I love you.

— Charlie.

Chapter 2
Prayer? Nothing To It

The standard first step when you are tackling any complex topic is to define terms. With prayer, that seems like a funny thing to do because everybody knows what prayer is. Even a little child will tell you that prayer is "when you're talking to God." And amazingly, that little child's definition may prove to be agreeable to a wide variety of human beings in all kinds of religions in all parts of the world. From the most simple minded among us to well-known religious leaders, prayer is when you're talking to God. Of course, just to keep any one set of words from fitting everybody, someone is sure to point out that *listening* to God is as important as talking to God.

Okay, okay. No definition is going to stand long for a topic with which so many people are intimately involved. Even so, we can move pretty quickly beyond the definition to the description. That's where the real diversity comes up, anyway. While most of us can agree on what prayer is, there must be a hundred thousand living color versions of how prayer is done. Think of those impressive video shots of huge courtyards filled with the Muslim faithful, all facing Mecca and all rising and bowing and repeating words together. Contrast that shot with a solitary believer praying at the top of a mountain, or a person kneeling among the shoes and tennis rackets on a closet floor, or bowing beside a bed. Think of kindergarten kids butchering the words of a prayer they are trying to memorize. Or watch a single heart-broken youngster on a direct line with God, communicating with the wordless eloquence of giant tears over the lifeless body of a dead pet.

You can take a prayer field trip through the world and observe a vast diversity of prayer paraphernalia. Candles in churches. Beads in wrinkled hands. Trees decorated with written prayer messages of the locals. Special roadside altars where gifts of food and flowers have been placed to speed prayers along. You may even see mechanical prayer wheels with petitions written on them and operators faithfully turning them to insure that the prayers continue grinding their way toward heaven.

You used to be able to watch the television camera pan the faces during the pre-game prayer at a big athletic event. Some heads bowed. Some eyes closed. Others waiting in self-conscious boredom for that voice over the public address system to finish the opening prayer so two teams can try to tear each other apart. We have listened respectfully to the eloquently worded prayers of religious leaders. We have reflected thoughtfully as we watch the one millionth repetition of the Rosary by a humble widow on the front row of an empty cathedral.

Prayer is tricky. Since it is a matter of heart and mind instead of posture, it is easy to be fooled about when prayer is actually in progress. Occasionally, we discover that we have been praying without realizing it — or that we are miles away from talking to God even though our posture may indicate that we are praying. I remember being a member of a small group at a church retreat. In comfortable clothes and relaxed manner, six or eight of us sat around in a cabin sharing aspects of our inner lives. After an hour of this tender conversation, the group leader said, "Now, let's pray about these things." Someone in the group responded innocently, "You mean we haven't been praying about them?" It must be humorous to God when we suddenly jump into formal prayer language to address him about things we have been discussing together in the most casual language... as if he hadn't been with us the whole time.

The power that prayer brought to Jesus was not overlooked by his disciples. He prayed all night before he chose his disciples. He was praying on the Mount of Transfiguration when he was suddenly transformed before his disciples' eyes. He prayed in Gethsemane's garden just before the most important arrest in the history of the world. The disciples often saw him praying. They recognized his obvious connection with the Father and they noted the power that resulted. It is no wonder that they asked him to teach them to pray.

For many people, prayer is not so much a joyful opportunity as it is a daunting responsibility. It seems to be far more widely praised than practiced. We keep hearing that prayer has produced incredible results for others, but our own efforts may have been futile and disappointing attempts to make solid contact with someone who seems never to respond. We would like it better if prayer worked in real life the way it does in the movies... with all those burning bushes and instant answers and clear directives straight from the throne of God. But in real life, we ask, we wait, we wonder if we've been heard, and we guess at the answers. We seek a deeper, richer, more certain understanding. We get hints, nuances, and take tiny baby steps in what we assume to be God's direction.

Pollsters tell us that slightly more women pray than men, slightly more blacks than whites. But, when the crises of life fall on us, all statistics are off and even the most hard-hearted among us are firing off those "anybody out there?" prayers. Under the heading of "there are no atheists in combat" belong a whole lot of heaven-bound messages from people who suddenly need supernatural help and figure it never hurts to ask. Like the sailor clinging to a small boat in a bad storm, they are banging on God's door with a proposition: "Lord, I know I ain't been very close to you up to now, and if you'll just help me out of this jam, I'll try not to bother you again for a long time."

The ways that we have seen people do prayer are too numerous to list. The petitions and requests are as diverse as the prayer givers. But the reason we pray, the motivation behind every prayer I've ever observed, seems to me to be the same for all of us: we need God. We are desperate for access to God. We may have had all we can take of the hypocrisies of organized religion, but we continue to hunger and thirst for a valid connection with God... a relationship that will give us a reason for carrying on with optimism.

Father,

Please protect me from distorting as I try to simplify. I am convinced that there are some ways to look at prayer that can help us all to be more honest when we communicate with You. But, as I try to grasp and explain those unfamiliar perspectives, please guard me from any words that might hinder. Make servants of my words and ideas, Father. Only servants. Servants that glorify You. I love you.
— Charlie.

Chapter 3
All I Really Want Is Everything

Asking God for goods or services that we cannot get any other way is one of the oldest forms of prayer. It's the kind of prayer that grown-ups tell us about when we are little. Or at least, it's the aspect of prayer that really sticks in our minds when grown-ups talk about prayer. That's because as beginning humans, we are instinctively selfish. In fact, some humans have been known to continue this trait well beyond childhood.

Talk to a little person. Tell him or her all you know about the mature forms and spiritual purposes of prayer. When you have finished talking, you can be sure that the part of your lecture that will be remembered is that "praying is how you get stuff that you can't get any other way." It's no surprise. When newcomers to the Bible read the life of Jesus, two stories that make big impressions are the two where Jesus feeds thousands of hungry people with only a few biscuits and some sardines. Even when old-timers read the book of John, one of the lines that sticks in their minds after the others verses have sifted away is Jesus saying to his disciples, "Whatsoever you ask the Father in my name will be given to you."

A friend told me about sitting with her young

daughter to discuss God's willingness to answer prayer. The daughter was skeptical. "Mom," said the little girl, "I have been praying hard every night for God to give me a horse, but he doesn't do it." Mom made her best attempt to explain that God knew the little girl had no stable for a horse, and maybe God was holding off on the horse until later. "It didn't satisfy my daughter," the mom recalls, "and I have just as much trouble today remembering that God is looking at the whole puzzle when he answers 'no' about some small piece of the puzzle that I happen to be praying about."

I have occasionally heard people explain God's failure to deliver items requested in prayer by suggesting that the prayer was for selfish purposes... or for mere physical comfort, or was just plain inconsequential when compared to the big issues facing the God of the universe. But that's not the kind of God we saw when Jesus came to live among us. Jesus showed us a God who understood and was moved by people's needs, a God who created and therefore understood, a God who had a "first person perspective" for every human being. Jesus also showed us a God who valued the human body and was constantly overcoming its hunger and thirst and curing its diseases. And Jesus made it quite clear that even while God is overseeing the comings and goings of stars and planets, he still takes the time to count the hairs on heads and note each tiny sparrow as it lights upon the ground.

Fortunately, it is not our job to know exactly which items of prayer are big enough for God to deal with. Our only responsibility is to spill our guts to the Father and let him decide what to handle. Soon after Kay and the boys and I moved into our house, we had several financial reverses. I reached the point that I was constantly worrying that we might be unable to make our mortgage payments. We might suffer the embarrassment of losing our new home. I worried about it a lot until the day I was jogging in the hot sun and prayed, "Okay, God. It's your house anyway. We are trying to use the thing in ways we think you approve of. So, if you want us to stay in that house, then please send the mortgage money our way every month. When the money doesn't come, I'm ready to move out of your house." I never worried about that monthly payment again and we will soon be making the final payment on that thirty-year loan.

I suspect that more often than not, when we approach God to ask for things we are using too much of our own judgment on just how big an answer he is able or willing to give. In the epistle to the Christians at Ephesus, Paul indicated that God is able to handle our biggest request... and then some. Paul said, "Now to him who is able to do immeasurably more than all we ask or imagine, according to his power that is at work within us, to him be glory in the church and in Christ Jesus throughout all generations, for ever and ever. Amen!" (Eph. 3. 20-21)

Instead of articulating to God only those needs and desires that we think we can handle, and then trying to accomplish them ourselves, we have to demonstrate the validity of our faith and trust by occasionally requesting bigger things than we can even imagine coming true. If we only pray for things that we can accomplish ourselves, how will we know God did it? Unlike the general who was known for saying, "Trust in God, boys, but keep your powder dry," we have to be willing to trust in God even when we don't have any powder.

It's probably impossible to escape the selfish aspect of prayer. Little children and spiritual giants both turn to God to try and get what they cannot get by their own powers. Little children ask for ponies, baby brothers, and candy canes because those are the things they want. Grown-ups are more likely to explain condescendingly that they are too spiritually mature to pray for such selfish things, and then go after their own good feelings by articulating prayers in behalf of more noble-sounding causes and effects. The child wants a pony; the grown-up wants to feel superior. They are both turning to God for what they can't get on their own. When Jesus told his disciples that entering his kingdom would require childlikeness, he may have been describing the wonderful childish freedom to simply tell God what we want without having to constantly analyze our motives, second guess our terminology, or agonize over His ability to deliver.

> God.
>
> *I'm sure you had a good reason for inventing selfishness, but it seems to me that half of my spiritual life is spent trying to root out something that you built into me. My natural, self-centered view of everything turns up behind every stupid, ungodly thing I do. The truth is, Lord, that at my dumbest, most selfish times, I would really rather control my own life than listen to you. But when I stop to think how often my short-sightedness screws everything up, I realize that I am in desperate need of somebody*

smarter than I am to run my life. Please take over, Lord. My way is just not working. Thank you for loving me in spite of my deep-seated selfishness..
— Charlie.

Chapter 4
What's the Deal Here, God?

The word for prayer comes from an old Latin word that means "to obtain by begging" and most of us have not progressed far beyond that initial concept. Some of us ask for ponies. Some of us ask for world peace. Some of us ask in faith, fully expecting delivery from God. Others just ask because there doesn't seem to be anywhere else to turn. Asking is a snap. The problem occurs when we don't get what we asked for. What are we to say when God fails to come across with the goods or services we are begging for? What does that do to our faith?

Are we honest enough to grumble that God claims to be our loving father but refuses to give us the specific things we ask for? If we had the guts to talk straight with God, we might hear ourselves demanding an explanation of Jesus' words in Matthew 7. "Ask and it shall be given you," he told his audience. "Seek and you shall find. Knock and it shall be opened unto you." Yet, here we are, asking and not receiving… seeking and not finding. And we want to know, "What's the deal here, God? Is this a promise or not? Can we trust you or not?"

It's a conversation that rings a familiar bell for

anyone who has ever raised children. There is evidently a legalism chromosome that is naturally resident in every child's chemical makeup, a chromosome that endows the child with an uncanny ability to spot a parental promise in the midst of the most innocent and generic parental statement. A kid who cannot remember anything else will zero in on that parental promise, store it away indefinitely, and then whip it out of the mental file just in time to turn it into a thumb-screw for obtaining whatever the kid wants. The accusation "You promised!" is the nuclear warhead in the arsenal of weapons kids use against their parents.

A charge of promise-breaking is enough to reduce many a resolute parent to a mass of quivering submission. Sometimes, this promise predicament is simply the result of some foolish and short-sighted talk. We promised something we shouldn't have and we are now stuck with a compulsion to deliver. Other times, the problem results from the child's misunderstanding or misapplication of the promise he or she thought was given. In this case, the poor parent struggles to explain the real intent of the words that were spoken while the child listens with closed mind and pouty lip.

Wonder which is the case with that classic "ask and you shall receive" promise? Did Jesus just get carried away by the enthusiastic attentiveness of his listeners at the sermon on the mount and make a rash promise that was going to embarrass God for centuries to come? Or did the young rabbi from Nazareth make a spiritually accurate statement which generations of Christians have jerked out of context, fashioned into a divine promissory note, and tried to collect on, year after year?

The situation becomes clear as soon as you start trying to imagine a world in which God turns his people loose with the power to instantly receive whatever they ask in prayer. It would be a world where farmers are praying for rain as picnickers are praying for sunshine, where hospital workers are praying for continued employment as sick people are praying themselves right out of hospitals, where environmentalists and land developers are praying patches of land from woodlands into shopping centers and back into virgin forests. The sun would flash on and off erratically as people alternately prayed for a little more daylight or a few more minutes to sleep. It would be a world of chaos, a world out of control, a world with all the consistency of human whim.

A little time in the trenches of parenthood helps to clarify the "ask and you shall receive" dilemma. You *do* want your child to ask for what he wants. You *do* want her to communicate continuously about her wishes and desires. If your child asks for something that you can give without endangering the child or the stability of that child's world, you give it gladly. But, if the child is asking for something that you know will be hurtful, you will be reluctant to deliver on the request. You will do what is good for the child: granting requests sometimes, denying them other times, and always nurturing toward the day when the child will be mature enough to say, "This is what I want... but I have learned over time that you always know best, so now that you know my wish, I'll leave it with you to give me what's really best for me." Or, as our perfect prayer role model phrased it: "Not my will, Father, but yours be done."

When our three boys were growing up, I tried to

make sure they realized the difference between their wants and their needs. Like most children, they would present any desire by saying "Dad, I *need* this." I made it my automatic response to ask, "Do you really need it or do you just want it?" After a while, they were correcting themselves in mid-sentence. "Dad, I really *nee-uh-want* this."

I wasn't trying to make neurotics out of them. I just thought it was an important distinction that they needed to learn to make. As their father, I did want to know both their needs and wants. And just because something was a want and not a dire need did not mean they weren't going to get it. But I wanted them to recognize the difference. And I think it's likely that my heavenly Father would appreciate it if I came to him with a clear understanding of the want and need nature of the things I pray for.

In his book *Your God Is Too Small*, J.B. Phillips gives names and personalities to several of the common human perceptions of God. One of the most haunting descriptions is the version of God that Phillips refers to as the "cosmic bellhop." The name says it all. It is a childish perception of God: a celestial being totally dedicated to your individual service, an omnipotent creator rushing about frantically trying to meet your every wish, an omniscient one hurrying to supply your every request, all in the hope of receiving a tip — a token gratuity for services rendered. "Get me everything I ask, God," says the worshipper of the cosmic bellhop, "and I will reward you with my regular church attendance and perhaps by doing a good deed now and then!"

So... what is the prayer regimen required to get on

God's good side, to get him to give us the things we want? Will a prayer a day keep the devil away? Is more prayer time required by city dwellers than by country folk? How often do we need to pray to get the benefits that God has for us? If we really believe that God is running a "you-do-this-and-I'll-do-that" game, we are sure to be disappointed. Our Bible role models put in a lot more hours praying than most of us are willing to spend. And if there were a clear one-to-one relationship between the number of hours we pray and the number of good things that come to us, there would be little need for Christians to preach Christianity. The word would have gotten around. People would be praying as dependably as we now see them taking their vitamins and making their insurance payments.

It is pretty clear when we read scriptural accounts of the earliest Christians, that most of them continued the prayer routines that had characterized the Jewish society. The Jews prayed at 6:00 a.m. (the first hour), at 9:00 a.m. (the third hour), at 12 noon (the sixth hour), at 3:00 p.m. (the ninth hour), and at 6:00 p.m. (sundown). In Acts 3:1, we read of Peter and John going to the temple "at the hour of prayer, the ninth hour." In Acts, chapter ten, we see Peter in one town praying on a housetop "at the sixth hour of prayer" and Cornelius, a Roman who had probably been converted to Judaism, "keeping the ninth hour of prayer" in another town. God speaks to both Peter and Cornelius concerning the same matter.

Should you and I be keeping all these various hours of prayer because many of the New Testament Christians kept them? Clearly, the answer is yes — if that's what helps. God has repeatedly emphasized throughout the Old and New Testaments that his interest is in the heart of the worshipper rather than the number of gold stars on the worshipper's prayer card. So in addition to our wonderful ability to send off instantaneous messages to the Father, we each need to determine the times and approaches to prayer that will meet our personal needs.

Dear Father.

I believe you have the power to do anything. But I can't get a clear fix on just when and how much of that power you intend to parcel out for my benefit. I see things happen as results of prayer. I see other things denied in spite of fervent prayers. I don't see a formula to it, Lord, but the longer I live and the more experience I have, the less I think you ought to entrust miraculous power to us humans. We'd sure love to control miraculous power so we could live less by faith and more by sight, but we're just too short-sighted. I'm afraid we would call down fire from heaven when we ought to be quietly suffering persecution. Thank you for being God, for knowing what's best for me, and for guiding as a loving father. I love you so much.

— Charlie.

Chapter 5
"Plunk Your Magic Twanger, Froggy!"

In the Dark Ages before television, I used to have a favorite Saturday morning radio show that featured a mischievous character named Froggy the Gremlin. The plots for most of those Saturday morning spell-binders revolved around the fact that Froggy had a magic wand that he could use to fix problems and avoid unwanted outcomes. We faithful listeners knew that all the problems were about to be solved when we heard the program's host call out dramatically, "Plunk your magic twanger, Froggy!"

That command would be followed by a "boiiiing!" sound effect and we listeners in radio-land would be told how Froggy the Gremlin had magically made everything all right. Whether it is Froggy's magic twanger, Superman's great strength, or some other hero's problem-solving wisdom, we grow accustomed to supernatural intervention to solve things we can't seem to solve for ourselves.

It always happens in the movies. We might begin to wonder why it doesn't happen just as predictably in our daily lives. I once overheard a little preschool girl in our neighborhood eloquently express this great human dilemma. As she struggled to solve some insurmountable problem at play, she sighed, "There's just never a magician around when you need one!"

She was right, of course. When things don't go to suit us, there's never a sympathetic magician around to whip the world back into shape for us. But for some who trust him enough to ask, God is not only willing and able to be the magician-on-call, he appears to be busily at work tending to the smallest of wishes.

For every person I have met who is puzzled by the fact that they prayed and did not receive, I have met another person who claims to have gotten the specific results they requested in prayer. Nearly a third of those interviewed by pollsters attribute their faith in God to the fact that they ask and *do* receive. They experience inner peace and a sense of being personally led by God precisely because their prayers have been answered, sometimes dramatically, sometimes in the most routine ways.

They prayed for God to clear up their teenage skin blemishes... and the blemishes went away. They prayed for a better job... and miraculously, another job appeared. They prayed for a good parking place... and there it was. They asked God's guidance in choosing between a move to St. Louis and a move to Philadelphia... and, presto! unsolicited information about Philadelphia arrived in the next mail. They took it as clear evidence that God not only answers prayer but was calling them to Philadelphia. For some people, the cosmic bellhop starts cars that have weak batteries and fixes television sets that are on the blink.

I must admit my skepticism about this kind of no-job-is-too-small God. I don't doubt the confidence of those who think God tended to those small details of their lives. I do suspect that the parking place prayers they remember to tell you about are the ones that produced parking places. I think they just forget to remember the times when their parking place prayers didn't work.

For me, the hardest part about talking with folks who think God is manipulating the world in answer to their smallest prayers is that they won't have it any other way. I am a curious kind of guy. I want to hear about their experiences but I also want to hear from persons who completely doubt that God grants such specific requests. However, the people who perceive God as always on call want me to agree with them that there are no coincidences and that God will do whatever we ask. Unless I am able to agree with them 100 percent, they are likely to toss me quickly into the trash basket they reserve for "people who just don't *really* believe in prayer."

I find it very frustrating that people's accounts of what happened when they prayed vary so widely. Do you suppose that God's answers to prayers vary that widely? Does he sometimes give personal service and sometimes keep his distance? Or is the wide variation of results more a matter of the wide variation of people telling the stories?

Just when I think I'm getting a fix on God's policy for responding to prayers, I run into another account that pushes me back toward uncertainty. For example, every so often there is a report from some physician who conducts an experiment, asking his or her patients to pray regularly for God's help in their recoveries. The statistics often indicate that a higher than normal percentage of the praying patients had rapid recoveries.

"Well, sure they got better faster than those who do not pray," I tell myself, "but do they get better faster than patients who might spend an equal amount of time in plain old stress-reducing meditation, with no religion involved?" Do tumors and blockages pop in and out of x-rays depending solely on who prayed last night and who didn't?

Then, just as I am getting close to a clear opinion on this medical intervention phenomenon, along comes a report from another researcher who asked non-patients to pray for a group of cardiac patients. But the puzzler in this new report is that, even though the cardiac patients were not told that the prayers were being offered in their behalf, they recovered faster than patients in an identical control group that received no prayers.

These kinds of reports leave me more frustrated than ever as I struggle to devise some dependable rule about when God answers "yes" to prayer and when he answers "no." Then it hits me. I'm going through the same frustration that would be experienced by a child trying to find the secret of when a parent answers "yes" or answers "no." The child keeps looking at *when* he asks the parent, or *how* she brings up the topic, or the *wording* used in the request. And, while the child is analyzing the asking, the parent is concentrating on the long term effects of the thing being requested.

I remember a clear analogy from my own teen years. I kept begging my parents for a motorcycle. My parents kept answering "no." I said I had saved the money and would pay for it myself. They said "no." I said I was different from other kids and would be careful. They said "no." All the time that I thought we were discussing motorcycles, my parents were really talking about my safety. Looking back now, I can see that there were no magic words or perfect ways of asking that were going to convince my parents and cause them to say "okay" to my repeated requests for a motorcycle. It was never a matter of how or when I asked for that motorcycle. My parents had a totally different view and vastly more mature understanding of the motorized object of my prayers!

In that great motorcycle debate, my mother and father were wise enough to answer a different question than the one I was asking. And so it must be with my heavenly father. He sees what I cannot see. He understands implications I do not even suspect. And in his love for me, God is very often answering a completely different question than the one I am so focused on. I am telling him what I want... He is giving me what I need.

> *Eternal God.*
>
> *Time is one of your most impressive inventions. The passage of time is a fantastic educator. My cumulative memory of the events that brought me to the present shows me every day that you are the father and I am the kid. I can tell I am growing and maturing. I can see my view of life coming gradually into line with yours. But I can also see my constant need for your guidance. Besides all that, Father, the constraints of time make me eager for the day that I can move into a realm without time. Everything I learn about you, Lord, just makes me want to know more. What a great God you are.*
> — *Charlie.*

Chapter 6
Thou Shalt Not Pray!

Let's pretend that tomorrow morning when your clock radio clicks on, before you are completely awake, you think you hear the following news item as a part of the early morning news.

And finally, in this morning's news, an item we're sure to hear a lot more about as the day goes on. Authorities in Switzerland announced this morning the long-awaited terms of the will of Herrick Hargreaves, the eccentric multi-billionaire who died at his Geneva estate late last month. Hargreaves, one of the world's richest men, had no living relatives and, by his own statement, no friends that he fully trusted. He has long been an outspoken critic of Christianity, which he once described as "mankind's way of running away from problems instead of solving them."

Well, it now appears that Herrick Hargreaves has found a way to continue his influence in this world long after he has left it. Lawyers disclosed this morning that every penny of Hargreaves' estate will go to endow a foundation that will work to demonstrate that, as Hargreaves often stated, "Christianity is a waste of valuable time and human resources."

Now, listen carefully because some of you out there in our Morning Show audience may actually be able to get in on the unusual windfall that this new Hargreaves

Foundation is offering. The foundation is willing to pay you $65 a week to stop praying. That's right. You heard it here first. This is $65 a week in addition to whatever you normally earn from your regular job. All you have to do is prove that you have been a practicing Christian for at least one year and then sign an agreement to stop praying. That's it. The Foundation will continue to pay you $65 for every week that you refrain from praying. It was Mr. Hargreaves' belief that within a very short time, the increased productivity of persons who spend more time working and less time praying will prove his life-long claim that religion is a tremendous drain on human time and energy.

Get your pencil now, because we have a toll-free number to give you that will put you in touch with the administrators of this unprecedented offer. That toll-free number is…

Okay. Back to reality. Herrick Hargreaves is a completely fictitious character and no matter how badly you need an extra $65 a week, this is only a made-up situation. But, made-up or not, it has never failed to provoke a fascinating discussion when I have presented it to classes I was teaching.

The whole point of the fictitious Mister Hargreaves is to confront each of us with the dilemma of that extra $65 a week: not enough to make anybody wealthy, but still a tempting amount that could help with a car payment or ease some other tight part of the budget.

For those who are not really praying much in the first place, there are some very interesting possibilities. A first thought might be, "Terrific! An extra $65 every week to stop something that I really wasn't doing in the first place. This is my lucky day." But on second thought, we might become a bit concerned about what our fellow Christians might think of us. That's when our powers of rationalization kick into high gear leading us to say something like, "Maybe I will just sign up for the extra money and keep right on praying whenever I want to. Who's going to know? It would serve that old guy right for his money to be wasted like that. I mean... can it be bad to lie to the devil? If this Hargreaves character was doing all this to put down Christianity, I'll just drain away $65 of his money every week. Maybe I'll even put the money in the collection plate at church. That would teach Mr. Hargreaves, wouldn't it!"

Just imagine. If whole congregations of Christians were to sign up with the Hargreaves Foundation and then toss the $65 into the collection plate every week, our churches might be able to pay off all indebtedness in no time! And they could still keep right on praying in private since nobody can really monitor private prayers. Right? Wrong! If old Hargreaves could buy our honesty for $65 a week, he would have won the victory he sought and would not have to worry about our prayers any longer.

It is somewhat humbling to stop and realize that though the temptation of $65 a week creates an interesting discussion, there are many times when we believers give in to temptation and deny Christ for a whole lot less. We may deny him — or shrink from speaking up for him — just to escape a bit of ridicule or embarrassment. No $65 reward for us; we just escape a few uneasy feelings. And in doing so, we may deny Jesus just as blatantly as Peter did on the night of Christ's trial. In the garden, Peter had pulled his sword and been fully prepared to die fighting for Jesus. But a few hours later he was unable to stand up to a little fireside ridicule. Peter's spineless behavior sounds painfully similar to our own occasional failures.

One of the first Bible stories that children learn is about good old Daniel in the lions' den. It's a memorable story because Daniel was faithful to God and the hungry lions never laid a paw on him. Unless you've read Daniel's story recently, you may have forgotten that the reason he was thrown into the lions' den was that he refused to not pray. A couple of politicians, who were jealous of Daniel's good work for King Darius, hatched up a plan to get rid of Daniel. They flattered the king into making a thirty-day law that if anybody prayed to any god, he or she would be thrown to the lions. The bad guys knew Daniel's habit of opening his windows toward Jerusalem, kneeling, and praying three times a day to Jehovah.

When Daniel heard about the new regulation, he went home to his upstairs room, opened his windows toward Jerusalem, and knelt in prayer where everyone could see him. His enemies rushed in, arrested him, and forced the king to carry out the sentence. The king really liked Daniel and stayed awake all night worrying about his friend in the lions' den. When the king went out first thing the next morning, Daniel was still in one piece and the lions were still hungry. Daniel explained that God had sent an angel to shut the lions' mouths and save his life.

I remember that as a kid my favorite part of the story was that after King Darius had Daniel lifted out of the lions' den, he had the bad guys tossed in. And they never even hit the floor of the cave before the lions ate them up. The final payoff in the story is that King Darius sent word throughout his kingdom telling all his people that he wanted them to "fear and reverence the God of Daniel."

It's a great story that we all remember. It lets us know without question how Daniel would have responded to old Herrick Hargreaves' offer of $65 to call off the praying. If Daniel would keep praying with full expectation that it was going to lead to dinner with the lions, he certainly wouldn't give it up for a measly $65 a week.

Only God knows why he saved Daniel from those Old Testament lions and then let so many faithful New Testament Christians be gobbled up by lions in the Roman coliseum. But the real point of this chapter is not lions. It is the value we ought to be placing on our privilege of regular conversation with God. With some of us, old Herrick Hargreaves is getting his way without having to pay a penny. Most people probably do pray when they come up against a major life crisis. When they run out of people to turn to, they turn to God. But, what a shame if God's response, when we show up with a desperate request, were to be, "Oh, hello stranger. Where have you been for so long?"

What are the odds that old Herrick Hargreaves' foundation is facing? One day, as I was speaking to a class of college students, I asked them to answer a few questions to give me an idea of their attitudes about prayer. My first request was, "Jot down a simple statement that will give me some idea of the frequency with which you pray." There were thirty-eight students who turned in papers. Ten of them indicated that they never pray. Six made statements that suggested occasional prayer. Six were honest enough to explain that they pray only when they "need or want something." A final group of sixteen students gave answers that indicated regular prayer habits... answers ranging from "once a day" to one student's slight misreading of the scripture that says to "pray without ceasing." That student responded, "As the Bible says in 1 Thessalonians 5:17, I pray *incessantly*." The Hargreaves Foundation may have its battle nearly won!

Prayer is to the soul what air is to the body. I must breathe, or my body dies. I must communicate with my Source, or my spirit dies. I cannot breathe only on Sundays. I cannot breathe only at bedtime. Breathing and prayer have to be continuous. As with other truly valuable things in my life, I may have to confront the possibility of losing them before I realize how critically important they really are.

> Lord.
> The world is so noisy... and so demanding... and so visible. It muscles in and jerks my attention away from you. It makes me concentrate on its urgencies instead of on your realities. Father, I get the idea that this whole life experience is a matter of learning what's real and what's just noisy, confrontive distraction. Please help me to stay in constant touch with you. Make my communication with you continuous and uninterruptable, no matter what distractions life is throwing at me. You've got the goods, Father, and I don't want to miss out on real life while I'm concentrating on noisy counterfeits. Please help me... because Jesus loves me.
> — Charlie.

Chapter 7
What If I Pray Wrong?

I've talked to a few people who are very ill at ease when they pray because they are afraid they will do it wrong. They assume that somewhere in the cosmos there must be a list of rules and regulations for proper praying. They fear that if they are not careful they'll stray off the beaten path of prayer and commit some accidental flub that will cause them to be eternally lost.

If you have ever taught anyone to use a computer for the first time, you probably recall the built-in fear with which novices approach computers. They fear they will accidentally hit a wrong key, which will result in the implosion of the computer itself and perhaps the total destruction of all data on all computers from coast to coast. A teacher's first objective is to convince such a student that he or she can hardly hurt the computer. There are plenty of ways to correct wrong choices and the reset button is always there if you need to start over again.

It is a similar fear that can cause otherwise confident and competent people to ask questions like, "Do you think it would be all right for me to ask this in my prayer?" Or, "I wonder if it is appropriate to bring up such a selfish topic when I am talking to God." Or, "I'm not so good at all those 'thees' and 'thous.' What if I mess up and don't use exactly the right words when I pray?"

It reminds me of the unfortunate experience our youngest son had with baseball. Don had gotten pretty good at hitting the ball during neighborhood games. So, when it came time to sign up for the organized baseball league at the park, he was eager to try out. On his first time at bat on try-out day, Don hit a home run. His second hit was also a good, solid one. He was immediately chosen onto one of the teams. At that point, his new coach began to teach him how to hit, pointing out one-by-one the flaws in Don's natural hitting style. Don's hitting grew progressively worse as the coach made him more and more aware of things he was doing wrong. By the end of the season, Don was striking out every time he came to bat. He had lost his natural hitting ability in a tragic effort to hit perfectly.

In the same way that stern grammar teachers with their red grading pencils have made many of us afraid to express ourselves through the written word, church experience and public prayer leaders have often suggested to us that God only listens to perfectly phrased prayers spoken in carefully intoned, stained glass voices. Of course, if you asked any of those public prayer leaders whether God requires such proficient performances, they would probably be quick to confirm that God does indeed hear all his children, no matter how they pray. Yet, flawless church performances — and the fact that the most articulate are the most likely to be asked to lead public prayers — continue to convince some people that God must place a premium on human eloquence when it comes to hearing our prayers.

Perhaps no communication analogy is so helpful to us in understanding prayer as that of the parent and child. My own mental picture, since I have never been a mother or had any daughters, has always been that of a father relaxing in his favorite chair reading the evening paper while his little boy plays with toy cars and trucks around and under the chair. Even as he reads his paper, that father is aware of the child's playful chatter. He hears the sounds of engines and crashes. He hears the boy imitate the voices of the drivers. The father may even hear echoes of words that he himself has said when driving.

That father is monitoring every communication, even the ones that the child has not intended to address to his dad. But when the child does stand up next to his father and address a specific communication to him, we can be sure that there is a different degree of attention. The father puts his paper aside. He listens with care and interest to whatever the boy says. He listens also to what the boy means. And he even analyzes the boy's sentiments as indicators of the person his son is becoming.

We cannot imagine the loving father responding to his son, "Sorry, Son. I cannot listen to you until you are as mature as I am and can speak to me in perfect grammar. I have no interest in things you may ask inappropriately. Please, leave me alone until you have perfected your communication style."

We understand the accepting nature of loving fathers. And yet, it is not unusual for spiritual A-types to express their reluctance about praying until they have "gotten good enough." They want to wait until they have perfected their lives, examined all the questions, and learned all the answers before they approach the heavenly Father. Jesus had the perfect analogy for them when he said it's the sick who need the doctor.

Rather than rejecting his child's immature attempts to communicate, the loving father is more likely to give rapt attention to the child's words. If the youngster's message is childishly phrased or immaturely reasoned, the father will understand and make the necessary allowances. He will give the child an answer that is right for the long term, explaining it as much as possible in terms the child can understand now, sometimes having to resort to the simple truth that "You will understand the answer to that when you are older."

Consider two forms of communication that might occur in this scene of the father and the child. First, suppose that each evening as the clock strikes eight, the boy rises from his play, stands by his father's chair, and repeats the following words: "Father, you are very good to me. You buy me toy cars and trucks. You provide a nice soft carpet where I can play. And you listen to me when I need help. Thank you for being such a nice father. Amen." Every night at eight the father hears those exact same words from the boy. Right on time. Every word in place. And then the child returns to playing on the floor.

Or... picture another type of communication between the boy and his father. The child is playing with his toy cars and trucks. In the middle of his play, it occurs to him how much he likes the little yellow sports car his father has given him. He likes it better than all his other toys. Without getting up from the carpet where his little face is only inches from the yellow sports car, the boy says, "Daddy... I love you this little yellow car." Not exactly correct sentence structure. Not really a formal communication. But does the father hear it? Of course, he does.

Do you picture this father as liking one of these two communications better than another, or just appreciating them differently? Does he prefer regular, form-letter prayers? Does he prefer those spur-of-the-moment, instantaneous e-mails from the floor? The answer is "yes." What the father prefers is hearing from his child. The father will make all necessary adjustments and allowances required to translate and understand what the child means, regardless of what the child says. The father loves the child, because the child is part of the father. The father senses the growing love and understanding of the child for the father. The child is becoming daily more and more like his father.

But, before we leave this happy picture, let's look at the flip side of this communication situation. Suppose one evening the father accidentally steps on one of the boy's toy trucks. Mashes it flat. Once the child's tears and the father's condolences have passed, the boy is once again playing on the floor, but he is still mad at his father. As he plays, he mumbles angrily about his father's big feet that mashed his toy truck. But when the clock strikes eight, the boy stands up next to his father, puts on his smiling face, and repeats as usual, "Father, you are very good to me. You buy me toy cars and trucks. You provide a nice soft carpet..."

The father hears the words and recognizes that they do not match the look in the boy's eyes. How will the father receive such a communication? My guess is that he will receive it with love and concern. He will think to himself, "I wish my son would understand that he can tell me when he is mad at me. I know his anger about the mashed car will pass but I am deeply concerned that he is afraid to tell me how he really feels."

My communications with my heavenly Father have benefited tremendously from this simple mental picture of a father reading his newspaper as his son plays at his feet. It has helped me to realize that my heavenly Father is monitoring all my words and thoughts, even the ones that I do not really intend for his ears. It has encouraged me to send off frequent, instantaneous, and heart-felt e-mail messages to my heavenly Father. Spontaneous, single-concept e-mail messages like, "God, what a brilliant design for the body's hinges. Thank you for giving me knees and elbows that are self-lubricating, self-cooling, and still working after all the miles I've put on them." Or, I have said, "God, I just want to thank you for the banana. What divine wisdom in making a banana! The peeling, the taste, the color. Great design work on the banana, Father!" I have occasionally shot off a quick e-mail that says simply, "Father, thanks for inventing laughter!" And perhaps my most frequent e-mail to God has been, "God, what a sunset! What a breath-taking phenomenon! But, I guess, it takes one to create one."

Jesus often used incidental and spontaneous message prayers to God. There are frequent examples of him breathing prayers of praise and appreciation to his father in the middle of the action around him. In Luke 10:21, after the successful return of the men he had sent to preach throughout Israel, Jesus stopped to praise his Father for the divine wisdom of revealing the truth to babes while hiding it from those who presumed themselves to be wise. Jesus frequently paused to thank God for situations he had been brought into and for the way the Father was guiding him. He even breathed a sentence prayer of forgiveness for those who were nailing him to a cross.

The father-child communication concept shines new light on the familiar excuse that there is just no time to pray as we'd like. Have you found yourself complaining that you are so overwhelmed by duties and responsibilities that there is no time to pray? That's like the child with the toy cars complaining that he is so busy with his toy cars that there's no time for communicating with the giver of toy cars. If that child loves the father, the communication cannot help but happen. No matter how crowded my calendar gets, I always seem to make time for things that are essential and central to me. I must not treat prayer as a spare tire... something for use only in emergencies. Prayer is my lifeline to my Father.

Another thing that the father and son communication analogy has made abundantly clear to me is how stupid I am when I try to lie to God. When I know everything is not right between us and I spout prayer platitudes and truisms in a vain effort to pretend the problem is not there, I am being spiritually childish. I am like the toddler who hides his eyes and thinks you can't see him. God knows my heart. He knows if I love him. He knows if I hate him... even if I'm too cowardly to put such an embarrassing thought into words. Realizing this, recognizing how totally transparent we are to God, I have come to the conclusion that... praying is one thing I cannot mess up... so long as I tell God the truth.

God,

I am so thankful to have the all-powerful Creator of the universe for my own loving father. I really didn't like it, Father, when I was growing up and people kept describing you as a stern judge who was more interested in behaviors than attitudes. That judge they were describing was a grim, unloving kill-joy for whom rules were more important than people and punishment more characteristic than grace. I tried to obey that God but I sure didn't love him. On the other hand, the loving Father that I now know makes love easy and turns obedience into a natural by-product of gratitude. Thank you, Father, for being the God I can talk to.

— Your clumsy son, Charlie.

Chapter 8
Even Asking
for the Bad Stuff!

The older I get, the more I pray — but the less likely I am to tell God exactly how I think he should respond. I have lived long enough to see the long-term outcomes of prayers that I once brought fervently and repeatedly before the Father. In many cases, I did not get what I was begging for. In some cases, I did. In every case, I can now recognize God's wisdom in the outcomes. I have to agree now with the sentiment of the country music song that says "some of God's greatest gifts are unanswered prayers."

An unknown writer has described the clear understanding that only emerges from years of praying for our *wants* and receiving our *needs*. That writer has said:

"I asked for strength that I might achieve. I was made weak, that I might learn humbly to obey. I asked for help, that I might do greater things. I was given infirmity that I might do better things. I asked for riches, that I might be happy. I was given poverty that I might be wise. I asked for all things, that I might enjoy life. I was given life that I might enjoy all things. I got nothing that I asked for, but everything I had hoped for. Despite myself, my prayers were answered. I am, among all men most richly blessed."

Years ago, there was a job that I really wanted. It seemed to me to be the perfect job for my background and talents. It would mean more money and lots of opportunities to build an influential career. I was even encouraged to apply for the job by the man who was to make the final decision. He said very encouraging things about the great future that lay ahead of the person who got that job. He was very slow and systematic in his deliberations. While he deliberated, I prayed. I tried hard to convince God that I should have that job. I was trying to pull all the heavenly strings I could. I made frequent impassioned presentations in my prayers, outlining all the ways that the job would enable me to do good. I promised God that all the influence that went with the position would be turned toward honoring him. I used every form of persuasion I could.

Eventually, someone else got the job. I was crushed. But, as disappointed as I was, I would never have thought of explaining the outcome by saying that "God gave that job to another guy." I could not have said that because I was working under a double standard that I find to frequently characterize Christian behavior. Under that double standard, I always gave God the credit when things went the way I had prayed they would, but refrained from blaming God when I did not get what I had asked.

Even though that double standard seemed to be in God's favor, I now see it as intellectually dishonest and spiritually unfair. It was as though I took every opportunity to reinforce my faith when something happened that indicated to me that God was on my side and stepping in to provide supernatural help. On the other hand, when things did not go the way I had prayed, I would rationalize that this must not have been a decision where God really needed to be involved. It must have been a decision outside his interests — perhaps an area where I was supposed to be learning to guide my own steps. Looking back, I can see that my double standard was letting me do the same thing as the people who rave about God answering their prayers for parking spaces and overlook the times when no parking spaces appear.

Twenty years later, I can look back and say without hesitation that God was interested in that job situation, that he did listen to all my prayers and presentations about that job, that he appreciated, as a loving father, my childish communications about the job... but that he knew so much more about me and about that job than I could ever know. In fact, I now see that he answered "no" and delivered me from that job in spite of all my begging.

With the 20/20 vision of hindsight, I can hardly believe that I even wanted that job. I can see now that I was not at all suited for it even though I had convinced myself that I was perfect for it. The job would have taken me in directions that I can now see would have been harmful to me, to my family, and certainly to my usefulness to God. Long term, that job I wanted so much would have been bad for me. I thank God regularly for answering that prayer according to his long-term wisdom instead of according to my short-term rantings, ravings, and rationalizations.

Someone has said that a major turning point for Christians occurs when they move from trying to control God to letting God control them. It is a major leap of maturity when we have accumulated enough prayer-and-answer experiences that we hurry eagerly to share our thoughts with a loving Father without thinking that we are entering a debate with a parent who must be argued into doing things our way. There is a clear difference between talking to God in prayer and spending time with God in prayer as we listen for his wisdom.

If there is a place where you often pray, you might do well to post there the heart line from Jesus' exemplary prayer recorded in Mark 14:36. As Jesus ends a night of togetherness with God in the garden of Gethsemane, as he deliberates the divine wisdom of his own imminent death, as he sweats out the pain and rejection that is to constitute the turning point of human history, he utters words that are so familiar to us that we can easily overlook their power for us. Jesus begs God to "let this cup pass from me." He asks that he not have to die. Yet, having stated his own personal desire with power and eloquence, Jesus ends with words that reaffirm his absolute commitment to God. He puts every previous plea into perspective with the simple words "not my will, Father, but yours be done."

I want to recall those words whenever I pray. I want to remember Jesus' words and try to copy his attitude. I want to reach the point that when I pray about a job I will say, "Father, there is this job that I really would like to have, but I've been wrong lots of times before. So I'm just going to trust you to do whatever is best about this. As a matter of fact, Father, if you know that what I need more than anything else is unemployment, then let me have it. Much as it scares me, if being unemployed is what I need to make me depend more on you and less on my own earning ability, then I yield to your wisdom."

I want to reach the mature confidence in God's view of things that I can trust him to give me whatever he knows will be best for me. I won't hesitate to tell him my preferences. I do prefer riches to poverty, success to failure, ease to drudgery, acceptance to rejection, health to sickness, life to death. But I want the final line after each of those preferences to express my confidence that God is the Father who knows what I need, and I am the child who lives in loving awe of his divine wisdom for my life.

Taken to its extreme, such an attitude will mean that prayer will cease to be a device by which I try to protect my life and obtain good things for it. Prayer will no longer be something I do in order to get good stuff from God. Prayer will be a simple matter of child communicating with father, spending time together because of love rather than for the purpose of gaining selfish advantage, and willingness to accept whatever comes from the hand of my loving father.

> *You know, Lord,*
> *I have less and less to request when we are together. I am more and more prepared to accept whatever you send. I have learned that when You "bless" me with things that people around me assume to be disastrous, it's not long before I begin to see the wisdom of your gift. So, give me what I need, Father. Mix the rough roads and smooth ones according to your divine wisdom. But please give me, with each rough road, the wisdom and spiritual stamina to endure until your purposes become obvious. It is a great relief, Father, to realize that you're*

smarter than I am and that you're in charge.
Thank you for Jesus who taught me to say,
"Your will be done."
— Charlie.

Chapter 9
What We Have Here
is a Failure to Communicate

Like many of the things we do every day, communication gets little attention from us as long as it works. We communicate — or assume that we do — and rarely give a second thought to the dynamics of the process. When we have breakdowns in communication, we often thoughtlessly try to overcome the problem by talking louder or underlining more of the words instead of analyzing where the system broke down and changing our technique to match the need. Prayer is a communication situation. Perhaps a look at the basics of human communication theory can provide a few helpful insights for sprucing up our spiritual communication technique.

At its most basic form, a communication situation has five parts. There is a (1) sender and a (2) receiver. There is a (3) message and a (4) medium. And there are various forms of (5) interference that can get in the way of the successful transmission of the message. Let's look at them one at a time and see if we can identify their counterparts in prayer communication.

The sender in any communication is the one who wants to get some message across to a receiver or, sometimes, to a group of receivers. A public speaker before an audience is a clear example of a sender: clear, because all the sending is going in one direction until the speaker gets interrupted by a heckler, a question from the audience, or a sudden wave of frowns across the faces of the listeners. A person writing a letter is another clear example of a sender. A writer uses little graphic symbols on paper instead of using the spoken words of a public speaker, but is equally intent on sending a message. Message senders come in many forms in our world. Of course, this simplified first step of communication theory suddenly becomes more complex when you and I stand face-to-face and have a conversation. Suddenly we are both senders and receivers.

Who is the sender in your prayer to God? In the most simplistic version of a "now-I-lay-me-down-to-sleep" prayer, you are sending the message and God is receiving it. But as you grow and mature, as you discover the additional power of listening as much as you talk in prayer, that one-way communication dissolves into a far more powerful two-way communication. You and God are both sending and both receiving. The familiar spiritual term for that is "communing." Messages are flowing simultaneously in both directions. Sometimes, when no clear messages are in process, the silent togetherness becomes a pleasurable communication in itself. Discovering the simple fact that prayer is not always me sending and God receiving can open up exciting new experiences. A prayer in which you set out to listen more and talk less is a prayer with exceptional promise.

The receiver in any communication situation is the person or group of persons to whom the sender targets his or her message. What could be simpler? Why is it worth our while to consider receivers? Surprisingly, more attempted communications fail because of receiver misperception than any other single cause. If, for example, the sender mis-perceives that the receiver is interested in the message when the receiver has no interest at all, that communication is going to fail. In cases where a sender mis-perceives the intended receiver's attention span or vocabulary level or prejudices or motivations, the message sent is unlikely to find acceptance when it reaches the mind of its intended receiver. Great communicators never lose sight of their target audiences. From the beginning of their messages to the end, they remember the exact characteristics of their intended receivers.

When we pray, our understanding of our receiver is equally critical. Our perception of the God to whom we speak determines how we approach, what we say, and the outcomes we hope for. If I think I am praying to a harsh and unforgiving disciplinarian whose primary interest is the dotted i and the crossed t, I will approach with fear and trembling and not much hope for acceptance. On the other hand, if I am approaching a loving heavenly Father who showed himself to us in the form of a Jesus who hugged little children and forgave sincere and penitent sinners, I can send my prayer messages with joy and with hope of acceptance. As you and I mature, our prayer messages should also mature because our understanding of the father is maturing. And Jesus gave his followers a unique advantage, a special "in" with the father. Jesus urged that we use his name as we approach God. "If you ask anything in my name," Jesus said, "I will do it."

The message in any communication situation is the idea the sender wants to get across. The objective is an idea transplant. We want to move an idea intact from the sender's mind to the receiver's mind. In a perfect communication, the idea that is in the receiver's mind at the end of the transaction will be identical to the idea that was in the sender's mind before it all began. Messages, however, are at the mercy of receiver preconceptions, multiple meanings of words, and our human tendency to think one thing and say another. Mark Twain is credited with the familiar saying that "the difference between the right word and almost the right word is the difference between lightning and a lightning bug."

On the spiritual side, we finally get a unique communication advantage! In prayer, the message is protected. In prayer, believers can actually say exactly what they mean whether they speak the right words or not. Human messages are frequently misunderstood because words mean so many different things to different people. But in our messages to God, we have the Bible's promise that God's Spirit is present to help each believer say exactly what his or her inner yearnings are trying to say. No matter what fumbling words may come out of our mouths, God's Spirit will deliver the true messages of our hearts. As Paul wrote to the Romans, "...the Spirit himself intercedes for us with groans that words cannot express" (Romans 8:26 NIV).

The medium in a human communication situation says a lot about itself. An interoffice memo gives a message one level of importance. A video tape production about that same message will give it quite a different importance. And a speech by the company president to a gathering of the entire workforce says even more. The same message, delivered through a different medium, actually becomes a different message. Thus, the cliché that "the medium is the message."

We have at our disposal words, pictures, music, body language, facial expressions, copy machines, billboards, telephone, telegraph, television, telepathy, and many other mediums. But we run the ever-present risk of sending the right message via the wrong medium. Several times, I have been called in to write an expensive video production that would eventually be viewed by an entire corporate workforce when the problem that prompted the video could actually have been solved if one manager had sat down for a heart-to-heart talk with two or three employees. Right message, wrong medium.

Another frequent mistake in the use of mediums occurs when senders assume that successful communication has taken place just because a medium has been used. This is best demonstrated in the familiar corporate question, "But how could you not know about the meeting? I sent you a memo about it!" A medium is just a way of transporting a message. A medium that carries the message only as far as the receiver's in-box is the wrong medium. Effective communication is a matter of selecting the medium that will carry the message all the way into the mind of the targeted receiver.

Here again, God is on our side as we try to select mediums by which we will communicate with him. Because of his power, mediums are not a problem. God doesn't waste time with the fallible media of human communication. He makes them non-factors of spiritual communication, specializing instead in listening to hearts. What a relief! No need to worry about selecting the right medium to span the realms between us and God. He is interested. He is tuned to the frequency of your thoughts and mine. He is listening. If we think it, God has the message. Just the level of communication expertise you might expect from the architect of the universe!

The fifth component of any human communication situation is interference. We understand interference easily when the medium of communication is electronic. We know how radio or television static can interfere with our ability to receive messages intended for us. Or picture a husband and wife trying to discuss something in the middle of crying babies, boiling pots on the stove, and other household distractions. Of course, interference can be mental as well as auditory. Consider the interference that exists when you try to send a message to a receiver who is already so prejudiced against your position that nothing you say is going to get through.

What role does interference play in my prayer communications with God? Clearly, my role as a sender or a receiver is subject to all sorts of distractions and environmental interference. Noises attack my ears and unrelated thoughts keep pushing into my mind as I try to communicate with my heavenly father. I can control some interferences by choosing the right time and place to pray. I can deal with some of the distracting thoughts. But the battle is never won. It will continue until I stand in the presence of God. Then, I feel confident that all my former distractions will fade away.

On God's side of our communication transaction,

I can only imagine one situation in which my father might be troubled by interference. While the designer of the universe certainly has the power to exclude external interferences, it must be painful to him whenever he hears me sending a prayer message that is different from the truth he reads in my heart. Whenever I try to lie to my heavenly father, I create my own spiritual communication interference.

I think that one of the main messages Jesus came to earth to deliver is that if there's interference between me and God, it exists on my side of the relationship. When Jesus told the parable that mankind has named "The Prodigal Son," he was not talking about the boy in the story as much as he was describing for us the patient, unfailing love of that wayward boy's father. I think Jesus was telling me that, like the long-suffering father in the parable, my heavenly father is always waiting for me to clear out the interference and get back to clear and honest spiritual communication with him.

Perhaps one other component of successful communication ought to be mentioned, even though it is not one of the traditional five components of the communication process. Preparation is equally necessary for effective human communication. Even though toddlers and other beginning communicators are able to make themselves understood, we still recognize that some people are especially good at communication because they prepare carefully for it and constantly upgrade their skills. In every situation, they focus on senders, receivers, messages, mediums, and interferences. They prepare the communication environment. They refine their messages. They study their receivers. And they remember to listen as much as they talk.

Preparation is especially critical in effective spiritual communication. Trying to grow spiritually on quick e-mails and emergency telegrams to God is like trying to maintain a healthy body on fast food and soda pop. Meaningful prayer — extended, heart-to-heart conversation with the Father — is as much an art as a practice and requires preparation. How can we prepare? We can arrange the right time and the right place. We can search our hearts and examine our attitudes and motivations. We can think about God at length before we begin speaking to him. We can revisit favorite songs and scriptures that remind us of the depth of our appreciation, love, and adoration for God. And we can be prepared to listen as much as we speak.

Prayer is fundamentally a communication situation. By paying attention to the components of human communication, we can increase our sensitivity regarding some of the aspects of spiritual communication. However, many of us are like the old farmer who was approached by the county agent. The young man offered to teach the old farmer some new and better methods of farming. The old farmer replied, "Son, I ain't farming as good as I know how now."

It may help my prayer life some to sharpen my awareness and direct my attention to the sender, receiver, message, medium, and potential interference when I address God. But, instead of waiting until I can pray the perfect prayer, it is more important for me to get busy "praying as good as I know how now."

Dear Father,

Thank you for your special help in my communication with you. No matter how clumsy I may be at communicating with other humans, I have your Son's promise that your Spirit is my constant translator, that a portion of you lives in me and clearly communicates my exact feelings to you, even when I can't express those feelings to myself. Help me now, Father, to be open to your Spirit and to become as good at receiving your messages to me as you are at receiving mine to you. To know you is to love you, Father. And I do.
— Charlie.

Chapter 10
Remembering You Always in My Prayers

In the last few years, I've stumbled onto a very satisfying method of accomplishing one part of my praying. It's a technique I could never have imagined using in my younger days because it is an undeniably mechanical, ritualistic approach to prayer. Since I was raised in a church culture that pooh-poohed ritualistic prayers as thoughtless and rote, it has been a pleasant surprise to me to see how much satisfaction I have derived from using a literal daily prayer list.

It all came about quite by accident. One month, among our church family, there happened to be an unusually large number of people with sicknesses and other troubles that needed prayer. I really wanted to pray for each of them every day. Knowing that my memory was just not strong enough to recall all of their names at any one time, I did what I would have done in any other part of my life: I made a list. I wrote down their names on a little slip of paper that I could easily carry in my shirt pocket. At my planned time to pray — or when I had a free minute during the day — I could pull out that list and meditate on the needs of each person in turn. It seemed like a logical approach. And it worked well.

I cannot report to you that each sick person on my prayer list regained robust health or that each troubled life found its difficulties worked out. Some did. But the great discovery for me about making a simple prayer list was that I no longer suffered that terrible sinking feeling the next time I would run into someone I had intended to pray for. I no longer had to suffer guilt attacks because I had sincerely intended to pray for them but, in the pressure of the work week and the weakness of my memory, I had just forgotten.

To be able to honestly and sincerely tell a person in need of prayer that I have been praying for them every day has clearly been encouraging to them and a pleasure to me. Praying for them is what I had intended to do all along. The simple device of the prayer list now made it possible. I certainly don't picture God frowning as he listens to my prayers... scoffing, "If that guy really cared about those people for whom he is praying, he would be able to remember their names with ease." I trust that the father is more interested in my heart-felt concerns and wishes for these persons than he is in how good a memory I have for names. He certainly knows the limitations of my memory and understands why I have chosen paper and pencil to keep these persons at the front of my awareness.

Actually, paper and pencil didn't last long as the medium for my prayer list. It only took a week or so to realize that names were going to be continuously added to and dropped from the list. It became clear that my word processor was the perfect device for maintaining an up-to-date prayer list. Not only could I add and delete names with ease. It was also a simple matter to move names up the list if their needs for prayer became even more pressing than in a previous week. A quick printout of my computerized prayer list gives me a "memory" that almost never fails.

Perhaps a written prayer list is so elementary and obvious as to be insulting to some readers. But before I stumbled onto it, I had gone through a lot of years of being embarrassed and ashamed because I had forgotten to pray for people I had really intended to pray for. Since I have been using a regularly updated, written prayer list, I have felt nothing but joy and satisfaction in knowing that I have remembered them in prayer.

The churchy word for this is intercessory prayer. Jesus frequently interceded for others in his prayers. When Peter's pride was about to destroy him, Jesus told him, "I have prayed for you, that your faith will not fail you." Parents were constantly bringing their children to Jesus that he might put his hands on them and pray. The whole seventeenth chapter of John allows us to listen in on Jesus' intercessory prayer for his apostles and for all that would come to believe on him through the apostles' teaching. It should be especially challenging for us to realize that, in John 17, Jesus actually prayed for you and me. With an awareness that was not bound by the conventional limits of time and space, Jesus implored his Father to keep those of us who would believe in him unified with each other — unified because we are all dwelling in him.

When Paul was writing to one of the first-century churches, he would frequently open his letters by telling them how he always remembered them in his prayers. Those references used to bother me until I convinced myself that Paul might have carried around a little scroll listing all the people he had met and taught and wanted to remember daily in his conversations with God.

Even more important than the memory function is the way the prayer list has changed the focus of my prayers from me to others. The power of others-centered prayer is wonderful in its ability to reduce the normal self-centeredness that might otherwise dominate my conversations with God. Not only am I remembering the needs of others, but the seriousness and frustration of their plights very often put my own wants and needs into a new, more realistic perspective. The old saying "I felt sorry for myself because I had no shoes until I met a man who had no feet" is especially true in prayer.

Prayers centered on the needs of others have made me happier than prayers that concentrated only on what I wanted for me and my household. A friend told me the same thing in different words. She said, "Almost without fail, when I have reached the end of my rope and have fallen to my knees and said, 'Please help me, Lord,' the phone rings or someone knocks on the door, and I find a person who needs me to do something for them — even to just sit and listen to them. This always takes me out of my need and into theirs, where, ultimately, my own healing takes place... or at least I'm given some space so I can see things more clearly."

Once my daily prayer list had become a file on my computer, it was easy for it to grow. Not only did I continue to meet other people who needed prayers, I also was able to create new categories of people to pray for. The original list of sick people was soon divided into those who were sick or injured and those whose illnesses were stabilized or chronic. After a while, it became helpful to further subdivide the list of sick people with groups that I named "Moms of...", "Dads of...", "Brothers of...", and "Sisters of..."

One week, when our church bulletin carried a list of fifteen or twenty shut-ins, I added those names to my daily prayer list. Since many of them were unknown to me, I became involved in a program of visiting and meeting them. One visit a month does not work a hardship on my schedule but it is amazing how quickly I have come to know most of our home-bound members personally... and how different my prayers for them have become. Now, instead of being a simple list of names, they are friends whose lives and grandchildren and illnesses are a part of me.

Ever since Kay and I went through the accidental deaths of two of our three sons, I have had a special compassion for those who are trying to endure grief. One section of my prayer list includes those who are grieving. Before the list existed, I remember some embarrassing conversations in which I innocently forgot a close friend's loss of a parent or brother or sister. Now, I review them every day and ask that the power and encouragement of God might be available to them as they work through their grief.

One of the sections on my prayer list is entitled "Troubled." I add to this list the names of people who have shared with me their struggles with relationships at work, in marriage, in parenting, in their own faith. I cannot promise these friends that I can solve their problems, but I can promise to mention them daily to one who does have the power to solve them. This section is especially helpful in correcting my self-centered view of life. Knowing of the pain endured by others helps to quiet my complaints and remind me how blessed we are.

Three families that we know have had to endure the life trauma of having a family member arrested, tried, convicted, and sent to prison. I added a new section to my prayer list. "Prison" not only contains the prisoners' names but also the names of their family members who stand in equal need of daily mention before the Father. These people are in prisons too far away for visits, but not too far for a monthly note that my list reminds me to send them. I want them to know that whatever else is happening in their lives, one person they know is still praying for them every morning. Month after month after month.

A happier section of my prayer list is called "New Opportunities." It lists people I know who are unhappy in their jobs, who are looking for work, who have just started new jobs, or who are beginning other new phases of their lives. I also list in this section the names of my various business clients, praying not only that I will serve them well, but that they will be influenced positively concerning Jesus Christ during the time we are working together.

Also included under "New Opportunities" is a topic very close to my heart. I list in that section the names of books I have written: those that have been published and those that are still in search of publishers. When I was a young writer, I did everything I could to get published. I got nowhere. Finally, I began to say to God in my prayers, "Lord, you are the only one who really knows whether these things I have written can be of help to people. From now on, I'm just going to write them the best way I know how and leave the publishing details to you. I'll keep the manuscripts in the mail to the publishers, but I'm leaving it up to you to decide whether they need to be published or not."

It has been a wonderful arrangement. I no longer worry about writing just to please publishers or readers. I just tell it like it is — describe things as I understand them - and leave it to God to either get my books out there to help people or let them eventually die in the mail. I pray daily for the books that have been published and for the people who read them. I pray for the manuscripts that publishers are deliberating over at the moment. And I pray for the books that I am writing at the moment... like this one.

Every now and then, when I come across Jesus' words of encouragement that we should pray for our enemies and those that despitefully use us, I wonder if I should add another section to my daily prayer list and call it "Enemies." So far, I haven't added it because I can't think of any. That doesn't mean that I don't disagree with anybody. It does mean that when I am at odds with someone I would much rather list that person's name under a category that emphasizes the positive side of his or her relationship to me like "Family" or "Troubled" or most appropriately under "New Opportunities." From a prayer perspective, an enemy is a new opportunity. It is hard to keep thinking of people as enemies once you start praying for them every day.

There are also sections on my prayer list where I pray by name for people in leadership — of our congregation and our nation. I also pray for those ministering within our congregation and in various mission points around the world. I have a section that prompts my daily prayer for each member of my own extended family. And I recently added a section that I call "Long-Time Friends." It includes couples and individuals that we have known in many places over the years of our life, people I do not want to lose touch with. Daily review of those names occasionally prompts me to pick up the phone and catch up with one of those names on the list called "Long-Time Friends."

A final prayer list category that I have found very helpful is called "New Names I Want to Learn." When friends have a new baby, I put that baby's name on that list. When new people enter my life, I add their names to that list. Repeating those names day after day helps me learn them and avoid the previously common embarrassment of not knowing names that I should have known.

I don't know whether a written prayer list would help you or not. It has really done wonders for me. I update it pretty often, print it out, and take that printout with me wherever I travel. I have no way of knowing whether my prayers have gotten results for those who have been on my list. I do know that I feel better just knowing that when I promise to pray for someone, I really am going to do it.

Dear Lord,

I can't get over the way the list grows: the list of your children that I meet and want to mention to you daily. Their needs are diverse, Lord. Most of them have problems that are beyond human fixes. They need supernatural help. I have no idea what solutions will be best

for them but I consider it a privilege to call them to mind each day and express to you my concern for them and my belief that you can fix the unfixable. Give what is best for each, Father. And help each to see the wisdom of your answer. And thanks for loving me today.
— *Charlie.*

Chapter 11
The Ultimate E-Mail

When I was in college, a well-known preacher came to visit the campus for a week. He spoke in each of our daily chapel services and preached each evening at the church next door to the campus. Every morning, it seemed, as he was introduced to us in chapel, the person doing the introduction would tell us that the reason this man was such a spiritual giant was that he had the habit of getting up every morning at four o'clock to pray and study his Bible until dawn. At least one of the introductions made a point of reminding us that Jesus himself would often rise a great while before day and go out into the hills to pray.

I was very impressed and filed it away in my young value system that anybody who wanted to become a spiritual giant needed to be out of bed in the middle of the night and busy meeting with God in the inspiring quietness of the pre-dawn hours. It was a glorious mental picture I had for a while. There I would be, meeting with God as the world slept, becoming closer and closer to the Father... becoming a real spiritual insider... and enjoying a corresponding rise in the insightful wisdom of my words, which everyone around me would certainly note and admire.

It was a great idea until I tried it. The first couple of tries, I set the alarm for four o'clock and, when it went off, I must have turned the alarm off without ever knowing it. Later, I woke up at the usual time and felt very guilty for not following through on my plan to become an early morning spiritual giant. Eventually, I managed to actually wake up when the alarm went off. I had not realized it would be so dark in our house in the middle of the night! As I felt my way through the house, trying not to wake up the family, I banged my knee on one piece of furniture and my shin on another. It was not a very spiritual way to begin such a great project.

When I turned on the light in my office, I thought I had blinded myself. Eventually, my eyes adjusted and I sat down in my familiar desk chair. I had never realized how cold it could be in my office in the middle of the night. I tried not to notice a bill that was sitting there on my desk so I could make a phone call about it later in the day. I bowed my head to pray and could think of nothing but that bill. I opened my eyes, whipped the bill out of sight into a drawer, and started again.

I bowed my head and began to pray. A few moments later, I woke up and realized that the words of my prayer had lapsed into a soft, but not very spiritual, snore. I started again with my prayer but soon found that it didn't really take very long to say everything I had to say to God at that time of day. "Oh, well," I thought, "I'm sure it takes time to work up to the lengthy prayer sessions I have read about Jesus having. This spiritual giant thing is going to take a while."

Looking back on those pre-dawn attempts, I can now see that I had almost no interest in talking to God. My real interest was to convince myself and others that I was a good person, a spiritual giant, as the cliché went.

I do hope that God got a good laugh out of my ridiculous antics because I don't think anything else positive really came of it, except my rather uncomfortable identification with the Pharisees and hypocrites that Jesus fussed at so much.

What do we do with those high standards of prayer behavior that remain stuck in our minds after we read about Jesus praying all night, or about famous Christians who routinely prayed three hours a day? And then, there are those frustrating Bible verses like the one in 1 Thessalonians 5:17 where, right in the middle of a list of spiritual exhortations, Paul tells the Christians in Thessalonica to "pray without ceasing."

Paul was always telling young Christians to pray without ceasing. To the Romans, he wrote, "Be joyful in hope, patient in affliction, faithful in prayer" (Romans 12:12 NIV). To the Philippian Christians, Paul said "Do not be anxious about anything, but in everything, by prayer and petition, with thanksgiving, present your requests to God" (Philippians 4:6 NIV). And to the Ephesians, he made it even more challenging. "And pray in the Spirit *on all occasions* with all kinds of prayers and requests. With this in mind, be alert and *always keep on praying for all the saints*" (Ephesians 6:18 NIV).

Pray without ceasing? Give me a break! Here I am trying to think of enough things to say to God to make a prayer last a respectable length of time and Paul is telling me that I ought to pray without ceasing. The Living Bible eases my legalistic burden a little by wording it "Always keep on praying," but I am still left feeling like a high jumper looking up at a ten-foot crossbar.

I don't have to give a lot of examples to prove that our pace of living is hectic and frenzied. You probably own as many time-saving devices as I do and you certainly have discovered, as I have, that those widgets don't save a minute of time. On the contrary, they fool me into thinking that I can squeeze even more activity into an already full schedule. Where is the time in such a life style to pray without ceasing? Do I want to drive my car down the highway knowing that I'll be meeting other Christian drivers who may be motoring with bowed heads and closed eyes, praying without ceasing as they go?

Okay, okay. The only reasonable explanation for this "without ceasing" challenge is that it is not a literal requirement. It has to refer to maintaining a constant awareness of God as we go through the day's activities. While I do remember hearing that, back in the Middle Ages, they thought that one sign of a really spiritual monk was that he had bruises all over him from bumping into things while walking around praying with his eyes closed, I still think that even Paul had to watch what he was doing while he was earning his living by making tents.

The entry of e-mail into my life has helped a lot with my understanding of praying without ceasing. Electronic mail came to us along with the inter-connection of computers. It has greatly facilitated communication between friends and colleagues because it removes many of the dreaded steps that used to keep us from promptly answering our regular mail. With e-mail, you don't have to find a stamp. You don't have to look up the address of the person you are writing. You don't even have to labor over a clever and appropriate opening paragraph to get you into the discussion at hand.

You receive an e-mail on your screen. It is a message that includes a question or two for you to answer. You can take care of it immediately. Response is simply a matter of telling your computer you want to reply, typing in a brief answer to the question, and letting your magic machine take care of the rest. No stamps, no addressing, no worries about correct spelling, no sweat. No wonder e-mail has enabled so many of us to finally get our communications as up-to-date as we have always wanted them to be. E-mail has made it possible for us to communicate without ceasing.

E-mail got me to thinking about "G-mail." My intended messages to God can also be procrastinated while I worry about finding the right "stamps," "addresses," and ways of articulating the situation. I can put off talking to God about things that come up, put them off until the situation seems more appropriate for kneeling, for solitude, or for more religious sounding language. Or, I can realize that God is wired directly into my heart: maintaining a constant connection with my thoughts and feelings and fully capable of receiving G-mail at any moment. E-mail can go around the world, but G-mail can travel from one dimension to another.

Jesus was a frequent user of G-mail. He prayed at his baptism. He prayed when he was transfigured. He prayed when the crowds were too accepting of him and wanted to make him their earthly king. He prayed when the people just didn't get it and were too stuck in their own self-centered worldliness to understand what he was telling them about God. Jesus kept the line open to his Father.

One of the images from modern entertainment media can help us to picture a person praying without ceasing. Movie and television dramas have made us familiar with the tiny but effective modern communication systems that help people do their jobs. Television news anchors wear virtually invisible ear pieces that bring them instructions from the control room. Secret Service agents, undercover police, and astronauts wear devices of constant communication that are portable, wireless, and so small as to be unnoticeable. We think nothing of it when we see a Secret Service man suddenly place his hand over his ear and listen intently and then respond with a few words spoken directly into his lapel.

God has equipped us with communication equipment that is even more advanced. He has given us devices that are not just small, they are invisible. They give us the power of constant communication with headquarters regardless of range and climatic conditions. And God's communication equipment is not subject to dead batteries or technical difficulties... unless we refuse to activate it.

It would seem to me to be a form of healthy Christian game-playing for us to think of ourselves as secret agents maintaining continuous radio contact with headquarters as we go about the activities of our daily schedules. This does not mean that people will see us talking into our lapels or mumbling to invisible people. But it might well mean that as I walk down a city street, I am relaying to my heavenly control center a mental message like, "Father, I am approaching that place on Second Avenue where I am so often tempted into lust." And perhaps the response comes back through my invisible ear piece: "Take a different street. Don't go that way. You are not prepared to fight that temptation, but you can avoid it. Repeat: take a different street."

In many ancient, church-dominated cultures, people developed specific sentence prayers to go with specific activities of the day. There might be a line of prayer or meditation that was recommended for the farmer feeding his cattle. There were prayers to go with the baking of bread, the lighting of candles, the start of a journey. Perhaps you and I should develop such prayers, little G-mails we can send off to the Father as we sit down at our keyboards, as we lift the receivers of our phones, or as we start the engines of our vehicles. There is nothing wrong with habitual or routine prayers unless they become so automatic as to be meaningless. And, even then, who is to say that a meaningless prayer is of less value than the aimless daydreaming we might otherwise be doing?

Sometimes when I have a repetitive task before me, like collating papers or sealing envelopes, I repeat a specific prayer concern with each part of the task. If I am praying for you during my afternoon walk, I may mention your name each time my left foot touches the ground. Repetitious activities can be open opportunities for the kind of heart-felt messages we want to communicate to the Lord. Of course, none of us wants to become a religious nut, murmuring pious platitudes or going through meaningless rituals all the time. But most of us could enjoy a little more constant and direct contact with the headquarters of our eternal souls.

One of the most inspiring results of e-mail was related to me by a close friend. He lives a thousand miles from the home where he grew up, the home where his parents still live. Through the years, the letters between my friend and his parents have been sporadic. Letters seem to always begin with apologies for not writing sooner and they usually try to cover too much territory at too fast a pace. But in recent years, my friend and his father have both gotten e-mail capability on their computers. The result has been astounding. By communicating more often and more consistently — even with only a line or two at a time — the bond between my friend and his father has grown stronger than it had ever been before. Even when they lived in the same house, there were busy schedules and multiple activities to get in the way of honest, direct sharing of personal feelings. But a line or two a day of e-mail has broken the emotional ice in a wonderful way. "This e-mail relationship has helped me know my dad as I have never known him before," my friend tells me. "We can talk about feelings and subjects in short e-mail lines that we would never have been able to mention in person."

And so it is in our communication relationships with our heavenly Father. Long prayers are like long letters. They have their place but they lack the power of constant and continuous communication. A developed friendship with God takes time. It needs small talk as well as major speeches. The more often we talk to the Father, the closer we become. The more constantly we involve him in the events of our lives, the less we are going to have to explain in each prayer. The more we allow the Spirit of God within us to maintain uninterrupted communication between us and the Father, the more intimate and rewarding becomes the relationship.

"Praying without ceasing" changes from a task for my legalistic system of Christian works into something I cannot help doing. I find myself actually enjoying the relationship. I like having an understanding Father on the other end of an open line. When things are going well, I can share the joy. Or, when trouble appears on my horizon, I have immediate access to the best guidance and problem-solving available. Like the Apollo XIII astronauts calmly broadcasting, "Houston, we have a problem," I am able to confront with confidence the worst that life can throw at me because at the first sign of distress, I am sending the message, "Stay close, Father. This looks like a problem."

> God,
>
> *What a great choice of colors! I would never have thought of green for the trees and blue for the skies. If I had planned it, I would probably have thrown together red and yellow and given the whole creation the blind staggers. That's why you are God and I am the kid. Father, you do beautiful work and I love you so much. More later.*
> — *Charlie.*

Chapter 12
Might As Well Lay It On the Line

Real love sees beyond mistakes. One day I was mumbling about some goof I had made. I said to Kay, "You sure find out how dumb I am when I do something like that." My loving wife responded, "Did you think I didn't already know?" We laughed together over it, but later it hit me that this was one of the most beautiful truths of a love relationship: Kay is going to love me... even when I am dumb.

It's only in that kind of a relationship that brothers and sisters can do any good for each other in prayers. Suppose you and I had no relationship other than at arm's length. We only see each other happy and smiling. How are we going to pray for each other? We can only pray for the one aspect of each other that we know — and there's nothing that aspect needs. I think James' instruction for us to confess our sins to each other and pray for each other (James 5:16) is a significant verse. Let your mask down. If you want people's prayers for you to have some effect, you're going to have to let them know the real you, the one without the mask. You want people praying for you who don't care if you're not the fastest guy in the 100 yard dash or the prettiest girl in school. The glory of the fellowship of Christians, the thing that the rest of society would die for, is the level of friendship that lets us lay the truth on the line and know that our brothers and sisters still care.

The more I think of God as sitting in his heavenly control room with a clear view of what's going on in my heart, the less likely I am to try and lie to him. Have you ever noticed those rows of little television monitors at the security desk of a big building? Each of those monitors is connected to a television camera somewhere around the facility. The picture on the screen shows the security officer exactly what is going on at that camera's location. In some security stations with lots of monitors to watch, the job can become a real challenge. God, on the other hand, has no monitoring limitations. His omnipotence enables him to simultaneously monitor the hearts of every living person. His monitoring ability is beyond the limits of our comprehension. That's why he gets to be God and we get to be amazed.

Remember that room full of monitors at NASA's Mission Control when we were first sending astronauts into space? Imagine you are the cardiologist assigned to sit in front of the monitor that reports an astronaut's heartbeat. You sit there watching the steady up and down movements of the video graphic and you know that all is well with the astronaut's heart. Suddenly, the line on the monitor begins to jump up and down erratically indicating that the astronaut's heart has started beating faster and faster. You open your microphone and say, "This is the cardiologist. What is going on up there?" The voice that replies sounds a little forced and unnatural as it says, "Oh... nothing.

Nothing is happening. Everything is A-OK here." If that sequence of events did occur, you would know that it was time for you to sound an alarm. Either the astronaut is lying to you or the equipment is malfunctioning.

God's monitoring equipment does not malfunction. The heavenly monitor for my heart is accurately reporting my true feelings and motives no matter what kinds of lies I may be trying to tell myself or others. I may act religious. I may say things that sound religious. I may do religious deeds. I may succeed in deceiving the people around me. But my monitor in the heavenly control room is constantly providing an accurate read-out of the spiritual state of my heart. No matter how humble and sincere my words and actions may be, my heart monitor can be blinking a warning message of "PRIDE" or "SELFISHNESS." God always knows the truth.

Perhaps this heart monitor concept can help us understand why Jesus was constantly locking horns with the scribes and Pharisees. It must have been puzzling for Jesus' followers to watch this charismatic young rabbi from Nazareth carrying on such a constant battle of words with the recognized religious leaders of his day. They must have wondered how Jesus ever expected to get anywhere in the religious ranks of his society if he kept attacking the power brokers. But Jesus knew something that his followers could not know. He knew what was in the hearts of those hypocritical religious leaders. He knew that their religious activities were only for human viewing and that their heavenly heart monitors were flashing warning messages of "GREED", "HATRED", "PRIDE", and in some cases, "MURDER."

Jesus repeatedly tried to tell his audiences that he and his Father were more concerned with attitudes than with actions. In Matthew 7:22-23, we hear him telling them, "Many will say to me on that day, 'Lord, Lord, did we not prophesy in your name, and in your name drive out demons and perform many miracles?' Then I will tell them plainly, 'I never knew you. Away from me, you evildoers!'"

Even though he warned them — and us — it is awfully easy to buy into the common assumption that "seeing is believing" and "what you see is what is true." And so, century after century, good and evil have waged a war for the hearts of humankind. Many have been called but few have risen above the easy answers. In every age, the masses have believed in appearances. Only a minority in each generation has been able to see that the intangible is more real than the tangible, the unseen more important than the seen, the truth better than a lie, and eternal peace better than temporary pleasure.

It's not news to us that God looks at hearts instead of hairdos. But it is a concept we have trouble remembering in the midst of a culture where all the emphasis is on the outward person. I remember hearing as a child the classic Bible story from 1 Samuel 16 about God sending Samuel to Jesse's house to anoint a new king for Israel. Jesse kept marching out his tall, handsome sons and Samuel kept thinking "This must be the one." But time after time, God would reject the nominee and remind Samuel that he was not choosing by muscles or profiles... but considering the hearts of these candidates. When they finally ran out of hunks in the house and brought in young David, the shepherd,

God told Samuel that this was the one: the one of whom it would be forever said that "David was a man after God's own heart."

Even knowing that God is constantly tuned in to our inner most thoughts, we Christians often prefer the lie that assures us God can only see what people can see. We will follow the rules as we grow up in a small town where everybody knows us and where our inappropriate behaviors are sure to get around to everybody. But let us take a trip to the big city where anonymity is a way of life and we may begin to think that if our close friends don't know, then God doesn't know. Knowing full well that God is watching, we are able to convince ourselves that he is not. Nothing is quite so amazing as the rationalizing powers of a human being who wants to sin!

Once the sinning is over, we Christians come crawling back to God in prayer. We say, "Father, I just don't know what's wrong with me! I didn't want to do that. I didn't want to be that way! I hope you will forgive me. I don't understand what came over me." But, even as we say those words, what do you suppose is on our heart monitors in the heavenly control room? Is God fooled just because we have fooled ourselves?

Suppose I get up in the morning and I am so distressed and discouraged and emotionally down that the last thing I want to do is talk to God. Yet, out of habit or fear of confronting the truth, I open my mouth and pray, "Father in heaven, hallowed be your name. Thank you so much for this beautiful day, a day on which the mere thought of you brings glorious sunshine into my life. Every day is a good day with you, dear Lord. I'm so grateful that you have saved me from the misery experienced by those who do not know you..."

Does it make sense that God would be happy with a lying robot spouting clichés of praise, or would he rather I would approach him as an honest but troubled soul who lays it on the line and says, "God, the last thing I want to do right now is talk to you. Sometimes I just get weary of trying to please you. Being good is hard, Lord. I am sick of it. I really wish you could just give me a day off... maybe with a day's pass to sin without it counting."

Hearing unpleasant truth from your child can hurt, but it is the only way to help the kid progress toward maturity. Even though God is already fully aware of how I feel, my honest description of how I feel proclaims my absolute trust in God and my confidence that he loves me enough to understand and support. Furthermore, I benefit tremendously by hearing those words of honest confession coming out of my own mouth. It is as if God and I now both understand. I no longer feel like it's me against God. Now, it's me with a problem and God with understanding and a willingness to help.

Being honest with God also makes sin less confusing for me. I can give up trying to decide which of my actions are little sins and which of them are really serious sins. It is only from the human perspective that sins can be ranked small, medium, and large. I have come to believe that willful sin is about the only kind of sin there is. Church folks like to split hairs and talk about sins of omission and commission and we like to tell ourselves that certain sins slipped up on our blind sides and we just accidentally fell in. But the more I think about it, the more I realize that when I sin it is quite simply because I knew what God wanted me to do and, in a spirit of willful pride, I decided to do the opposite. It is a humbling realization. It shows me that at the moment I am committing some "small socially acceptable" sin my heart monitor in the heavenly control room is displaying exactly the same message as the monitor of the world's most socially unacceptable mass murderer. I think that in God's eyes sin is sin, rebellion is rebellion, and my willful decision to make my own rules is no different from Jack the Ripper's willful decision to play God with the lives of other human beings.

Is it possible that I should become so honest with God that I will find myself praying even as I sin? As I am waging some internal battle with one of my lower urges — and even giving in to that urge — can I be simultaneously on the phone with God? Would it be the ultimate blasphemy to be discussing my rebellion with God even as I approach or commit that act of rebellion?

I know from experience that it is possible. I also know from experience that this double-minded view of temptation can be an important step along the path toward stripping any sin of its deceptive allure. Continuing my communication with God even as I am committing some familiar sin has frequently been the beginning of the end for that sin. Trying to explain to God why I am making such a short-sighted choice can be the surest way to see that specific sin for the lying deceiver it really is. Excuses which sound quite rational within my own mind begin to fall apart when I try to explain them to God.

Laying it on the line with God about my sins

— even as I am committing them — places the whole sin transaction in amazingly clear perspective: I am the battlefield of a war. Part of me wants to sin. Part of me wants to refrain. If I choose the sin, its pleasure will be immediate, fleeting, and rarely as enjoyable as advertised. If I back away from this sin, the pleasure of God will continue to be eternal, permanent, and even better than I am now able to comprehend.

Seen through God's eyes, sin is really a dumb choice. This clarified view of the sin transaction can help me make the right decision. But it's a view of the sin transaction that is only available if I maintain contact with God even as I walk through the valley of the shadow of sin and death.

> Father,
>
> What a relief to finally believe that you know everything that is going through my heart, even the most ungodly of my thoughts. Your omniscience was such a terrifying thought back when I thought you were a stern disciplinarian eager to zap me for the smallest slip-up. But now that I know you as a loving Father, I can rest in your grace. I still want to clean up my thoughts, to make my heart more and more a place that honors you. But now, I want to do it out of love rather than fear. Thank you for being the God of love who chases away fear. Your love makes me want to love better.
> — Charlie.

Chapter 13
Shut Up and Listen!

This chapter is especially for me. The meditation half of prayer is one that I just forget to make time for. I read about it. I believe the promises people make for it. I've just got to find the time — to set aside, to dedicate the time — to meditate.

It shouldn't surprise me that listening should be the weakest aspect of my communication with God; it's the weakest aspect of my communication with everybody. Listening is a forgotten skill of our communication practice. The world is full of tutors and groups offering to teach us to be better speakers. But I don't recall ever being offered instruction on how to be a better listener.

Half the time when we think we are listening to what another person is saying, we are actually concentrating on what we are going to say as soon as that person stops talking. Listening is not just being quiet while our communication partner has his or her turn to talk. Listening is concentrating on the viewpoint the other person is explaining. I am not truly listening to your side of our discussion until I am trying hard to hear your statements with an open mind and see them through your eyes. I am not really listening until I am actually making an effort to see things your way!

In the spiritual realm, it is obviously necessary to shut up and listen, to arrange periods of time where I clear my mind of all its day-to-day clutter and allow a time of silence for my heavenly Father to have his say. And in the same way that I need to make an effort to get into your mind as I am trying to listen to you, I will do well to prep my mind in order to hear what God has to say. There are scripture verses that can put me more on God's wave length. There are songs. There are sayings and stories. I may even need to fast to really prepare to listen. Maybe I need to get in the habit of turning off that ever-present radio in the car so there's less noise in the air when God has something to say to me. All these things can help get me into the mind of God — to get ready to listen.

However, I know how I am. I know that reading things can often send me off on unanticipated tangents, generating more confusion instead of less. The last thing I need to do as I prepare to shut up and listen is to read something that generates a scriptural distraction to replace my worldly distractions. Given my personality, the greater challenge is going to be stopping: throwing on the brakes, cutting free from the compulsion to keep doing things, thinking things, making progress. I am going to need to seek out prepping techniques that will shake me loose from my own natural tendencies to keep chugging. Perceiving myself as doing nothing may be the highest hurdle I have to clear in order to spend meditation time with God. I must find ways to stop my nervous chatter and give God a chance to talk.

I am convinced that meditation would benefit anybody. The calming, centering, and life-renovating power of meditation is constantly endorsed, even by our secular media. Regular articles attest to the positive gains made by people who take up meditation: who take regular opportunities to clear their minds and follow the meditation techniques of one teacher or another. Yoga and a hundred other methodologies have their positions, mantras, and techniques. I say, "Whatever works for you, use it."

For myself, I love meditating in my one-button suit. Nothing disconnects me from the pressures of daily life quite like the total relaxation I can enjoy after jogging. I come back to the house after jogging through the neighborhood: hot and sweaty, my blood rushing enthusiastically to warm every corner of my body. I take a quick shower and towel dry. Then, I stretch out on the bedroom floor wearing nothing but the clothes I was born in. I lie there on my back, my arms flat on the floor, my eyes closed, consciously relaxing every muscle, and concentrating on my breathing.

Sometimes I repeat silently the simple phrase "grace and peace" in time with my breathing. As I breathe in, I think grace. As I breathe out, I think peace. It is an especially meaningful refrain for a person raised in a church fellowship that gave lip service to grace but placed its major emphasis on works. The day that I really understood that God was going to save me regardless of my works was the day I was set free from a law of sin and death. It was the discovery that first brought me real peace. And so, as I consciously relax every muscle and slow my breathing, I breathe in the grace of God and breathe out a peace that passes human understanding.

As I lie there, the most natural series of thoughts

occurs to me. I begin to think, "God, what an amazing creation is the human body you designed: the way the blood feeds the muscles, the way the muscles move the body, the way the systems work together so beautifully, year after year. Self-replenishing, self-cooling, permanently lubricated bearings. It is typical of your phenomenal creation. Father, you are one great God!"

It's a series of thoughts that provides a natural launch pad for further observations of sincere praise to the unbelievable designer. It would be the ideal beginning for a time of meditation if there were not so much I want to say! I must learn to interrupt my words by saying, "Father, you are so great. Now please help my brain to stop chattering to you and just listen."

> *Speak to me, Lord. Help me to take the time to clear my calendar and my mind, to make a place and an opportunity, and to listen. It's crazy for me to do all the talking when we meet. You are the one with something worth saying, something worth hearing. Help me to shut up and listen, Father, according to the example of Jesus. Love, from the big mouth.*
> — *Charlie.*

Chapter 14
Does God Speak Olde English?

I saw a bumper sticker that said, "If it's not the King James, it's not the Bible!" It was obviously riding on the bumper of a person who had a strong commitment to the unique sound of the scripture as it was first translated into the English of the 1600s. I wondered why the bumper sticker did not read, "If it be not of King James, it canst in nowise be approvéd!"

The truth is that God does speak Olde English. He speaks Olde English and all the other languages known to humankind... and then some. If we are impressed when we meet someone who speaks multiple languages, we should be overwhelmed when we realize that the God of all the earth speaks all 3,000 or more languages and is fluent in each of their dialects.

Since God knows perfectly well what I mean in my own style of everyday talking, does it stand to reason that he would be more pleased if I took the pains to learn an out-of-date language in which to address him? Would God rather hear me come to him saying "Despise not thine erring servant who cometh earnestly beseeching thy pardon and reconciliation," or is it more reasonable for me to come saying, "Well, God, I blew it again. Please forgive me again and take me back"? Does

God want me to have one style of talking to everybody else and a different style for him? If so, it would sure get in the way of my continuing conversation with him.

One aging dowager surprised her friends by taking up the study of Hebrew when she turned 88. When someone questioned her about this decision, she answered that she felt it was proper to greet her creator in his native tongue! The idea that God might have a native tongue is an interesting one that reveals some of our unrealistic preconceptions about him and our communication practices with him. These preconceptions often show up in our prayers. Indeed, prayer is a good barometer of faith. The way we pray often reveals what we really believe.

Remember our illustration of the control room in heaven? Remember the depiction of God tuned in to all the heart monitors of all the people in all the world? No human could accomplish that, but God can handle it. He is not limited to my thought patterns. He is not limited to the language I speak. He spoke the worlds into existence. Why should I worry about his ability to understand what I am saying? He's not the one with the understanding limitations. I'm the one still trying to overcome cartoon images of God as a little, old, cloud-dwelling gentleman with white hair and beard. My attempts to be honest and realistic with God will be an unending struggle to overcome the stereotypes of the media and the King James terminology of my earliest years in churches and Sunday schools.

A very perceptive teenager once asked me a long time ago if we would be reading the Bible in heaven. She was a new Christian and she had heard a lot of talk about the importance of reading the Bible and studying it every day. I'm not sure how I answered then but if I were answering her now, I would say, "Suppose you had a pen pal that you had been corresponding with for a long time. Then, one day you find out your pen pal is coming to see you. When the pen pal arrives at your house, how likely is it that you will say, 'I am so glad you're here. Please sit down while I read about you from these letters you sent me'"?

Obviously, we would be foolish to dwell on written descriptions when the live character is sitting there before us. By the same logic, the idea of reading the Bible in heaven is ridiculous. Why would I want to read Paul's epistles when I can just ask Paul about it? Why wonder any longer about the nature of Jesus or God when I can spend endless days in their presence? For purely realistic anticipation, I much prefer the attitude expressed by a friend who told me that the first thing he plans to do when he gets to heaven is to find Adam and punch him in the mouth for causing mankind to have to work.

And yet, I have known people who would be very disappointed if Bible study were not a major part of the heavenly schedule. For them, Christianity has become a matter of knowing every detail of the Bible. Some of them can argue at length about the appropriateness of one translation or another — about the difference that one word or another can make in our faith. While I grant that there are times when a little background on a word or a grammatical construction can deepen our understanding, it is hard for me to spend time haggling over one translation or another when the good news of Jesus Christ is designed to be as understandable to an illiterate person as it is to a learned one.

Another argument that Christians fall into from time to time has to do with whether prayers should be ritual or spontaneous. Some people prefer the written prayers that have served many generations of Christians and found their way into liturgical readings and hymns. Members of the written prayer club identify with the sentiments of these historic lines and take extra comfort in knowing that the ancient words seem somehow more holy because they have been around so long.

On the other side of the preference is the spontaneous prayer group. It is made up of Christians who doubt the intimacy of any prayer they didn't make up themselves. "What good is it to me," they would say, "If I am talking to God in words straight from the heart of Saint Somebody Else?"

The tragedy here, as in most religious controversies, is that both sides look down in pious condescension on the other. Instead of saying "I prefer this and you prefer that," they allow their opinions to push them into the corner of "I am right and you are wrong."

It might help all of us to remember that Jesus used both forms of prayer. As a good Jew, he went to the synagogue where scriptures and prayers were recited. He almost certainly recited the *Shema* twice a day and stopped his carpentry for the morning, afternoon, and evening prayers. And his spontaneous prayers recorded in the gospels spoke personally to God and served as examples for his listening disciples.

Letters to New Testament congregations quote numerous sayings that had clearly been adopted into the public and private worship of the earliest

Christians. Paul, who was known to include his own spontaneous prayers in his epistles, appears to be recommending to Timothy the increased usage of one ritual line of truth when he writes, "Here is a trustworthy saying that deserves full acceptance: Christ Jesus came into the world to save sinners — of whom I am the worst" (1 Timothy 1:15 NIV).

Another real hair-splitting discussion has been whether one's private prayers should be spoken or silent. To me, it is hard to imagine that there is much to discuss on a topic like this. But the spoken prayer lobby is fond of reading us the verses that show Bible characters praying out loud, while the silent prayer constituency questions the wisdom and sincerity of anybody who would verbalize prayers to an invisible, all-knowing God. As with so many of our preoccupations in religious discussion, we would be better off with no lines drawn, better off wishing Godspeed to those who pray silently, those who pray aloud, and those who find that they can pray better standing on their heads. My motto is, "Use whatever helps you get through."

Most of us have heard references to *Abba*, the most familiar Jewish term for "father." I am told that this word was the equivalent of our word "Daddy", a term of ultimate intimacy that a child reserved for a loving father. We are familiar with Jesus' use of *Abba* in addressing God but we less frequently notice that it was exactly this same familiar word with which Jesus began the model prayer he gave to his disciples. Imagine the shock to his faithful Jewish followers — people who were reluctant to even pronounce the name of Jehovah — when Jesus suggested that they start their prayers by calling God "Daddy." It was a new image for God: an image of a loving father who wanted to cuddle them close and hear their most intimate and continuing communications.

When it comes to how my prayers are worded, I am of the opinion that my loving heavenly father is less interested in what language I am speaking than in the care and honesty with which I express myself. I think God would rather hear a few words I have examined and thought through than a whole page of parroted religious jargon that comes rolling out simply because I started my mouth before I put my heart and mind in gear.

> *Dear Father,*
> *I just can't imagine how it's going to be. Everything I learn about the divine wisdom of your earthly creation just whets my appetite for the wonders you must have waiting in your heavenly creation. Amazement... wonder... shock... there are no human words, Lord, for the impressions to be revealed. I guess we'll be needing a brand new heavenly language too, just to comprehend the things you have in store. Come back soon, Lord Jesus. Let's do this heaven thing.*
> *— Charlie.*

Chapter 15
Do I Get Extra Points for Praying on Mountaintops?

Somewhere along the way through childhood, I got an overdose of the Hollywood view of life. It wasn't that I went to so many movies or even watched more television than the average American kid. It was just that whenever filmmakers depict something, they have the time and resources to do it in the extreme. In the classic scene where the good guy hero is having his patience pushed to the limit and trying to remain a man of peace, the bad guys beat him to a bloody pulp. The bad guys are so bad and the good guy is so good that by the time the hero finally gives in, unwraps his trusty six-shooter, and blows away thirty bad guys without reloading, you feel he is fully justified for all this righteous indignation and mayhem.

And at the ends of movies, when all the problems have been resolved and the audience is supposed to rejoice that the characters are going to "live happily ever after," filmmakers really pour it on. The sun is shining, the skies are blue, the smiles are pearly, everybody is laughing, and the music of a full orchestra is swelling to a crescendo that makes you want to jump up and celebrate.

The skill of filmmakers is impressive... but a little troublesome for those of us who have to live in the real world. The problem is that I want real life to go like the movies and it just doesn't work that way. For example, I read those verses that describe for me Jesus' habit of getting up before daylight, slipping quietly away from the snoring disciples, and walking up into the hills to pray. With the halo effect of Hollywood working overtime in my mind, I picture it all too perfectly. A little chirping bird greets the Savior and the imminent sunrise. Jesus makes his way effortlessly along a smooth path and emerges on a promontory overlooking the valley. Here he communes in prayer and meditation with the Father: getting all the answers, solving all the problems. As the first golden beams of sunlight streak across the morning sky, choirs of offstage angels raise their voices to underscore the perfection and victory of the elegant moment.

It is a wonderful picture... until I try to go up into the mountains to pray. To start with, there are no mountains within walking distance of my house. That means either a car trip or a motel bill stands between me and praying in the mountains. If that weren't enough, there are the irritants of making my way up to a proper spot for mountain prayer. It's dark in the woods before daylight! That means getting batteries for the flashlight and inching my way along the path as roots trip me up and spider webs wrap around my face. When I finally reach the promontory, there is no really comfortable place to sit. Kneeling hurts my knees and back and, no matter what position I try, there is always a sharp stone under me. On top of all this, I am not alone on the mountain; a pre-dawn squadron of gnats is circling my head and attempting kamikaze dives into my ears.

Praying is a lot easier in the movies than in real life. I'd like to get my hands on whoever came up with the cliché "mountaintop experience" to describe an outstanding spiritual event. Those words bring an impressive set of visuals to mind, but to my way of thinking also create unrealistic and unattainable stereotypes for folks like me. How must the term "mountaintop experience" make a poor plains dweller feel? And where do you go for a mountaintop experience when you live on 153rd Street with a view of nothing but dirty bricks and smog?

The inspiration of nature may have been greatly oversold in the past. It is certainly getting harder and harder to find in the present. A friend told me about flying into Canada on a fishing expedition. After taking a seaplane to an isolated northwoods lake, paddling a canoe across several lakes, and hiking overland to a lake of promised virgin splendor, my friend looked down at his feet and saw an aluminum tab from the top of some previous visitor's soft drink can.

It becomes clear pretty quickly that there is no running away from civilization to places of natural beauty that make prayer easier or more productive. Nature is nice; it can deliver its own inspirations and amazements. But those of us who keep searching for the perfect panorama with offstage choirs of angels are going to continue to be frustrated. The real world alternative is to find your places of prayer wherever you are and adapt them to fit your personal needs.

In my case, Jesus' advice in Matthew 6:6 about going into your own room, shutting the door, and praying in secret seems far more promising. I know that I need to minimize or even eliminate visual distractions to get anywhere with prayer. Therefore, mountaintop prayer sessions are going to be less productive for me than those in the dark of a closet or the limited distractions of a familiar room. Closed eyes are a definite necessity for me and any reduction of background sounds is going to be a plus.

God can receive my communications no matter where I am when I send them, but my ability to receive his messages needs to allow for my own high distractibility. It may require some doing, but necessary adjustments can always be made in cases of life and death. And my communication with God is far more critical than life and death.

One person I know created a tiny prayer room in a storage closet under the stairs of her home. Having cleared out the suitcases and other household junk, she was left with a tiny space that had a carpeted floor and plain walls. She put a few items there that would assist in her devotions but she kept them to a minimum. She quite literally entered into her closet to pray. Equally important, her prayer closet was always handy. She did not have to make a trip or rearrange the day's schedule to contact headquarters and refocus on her mission. And, as her place of prayer became more and more familiar, I would assume that the mere action of entering that closet would make it easier and easier to quickly assume an attitude of prayer. A friend who used to live in Scotland tells me that the storage area under Scottish stairs is referred to as "the glory hole" because of the unlimited mixture of treasures and junk that may be found stuffed in there. But, in a more literal sense, a personal place of prayer created in such a household hideout could become a glory hole.

Dear Father,

Help me to get rid of all those stereotypes and preconceptions that get in the way of my knowing you and your Son and your Spirit as you are. Like the sun burning off the morning fog, send your Son into my mind and burn off the clutter so I can hear you. I love you.
— Charlie.

Chapter 16
Do Kneelers
Get Preferential Treatment?

I grew up in a non-kneeling church. I don't remember anyone ever saying a word against kneeling in prayer but it was sort of understood that the only folks who might be seen kneeling during our prayers would be the more spiritually renowned preachers. Even as a kid, it struck me as curious that those preachers who kneeled to pray when they were up on the stage did not usually kneel when they were seated with the rest of us in the audience.

We had lots of prayers in our services but they usually occurred with the congregation standing or sitting with heads bowed and eyes closed. I remember as a little squirt scanning the audience during the prayers to try and catch people who were keeping their eyes open during the prayer. It was a kind of "prayer tag" and it never occurred to me that I was the first one caught every time I played it.

Occasionally, I would get to go to services with my friends who went to kneeling churches. I would be fascinated by the foam-padded kneeling rail in front of our pew. But... when we all kneeled on them to pray, my young mind was so busy processing this brand new kneeling experience that I never got anywhere close to praying.

Mine was not a childhood that provided much insight on the proper posture for prayer and I found myself approaching the writing of this chapter with a real lack of experience in prayer posture alternatives. "Oh, well," I thought. "No time like the present to try them out... as long as I make my trial runs in private so as not to scare my long-time friends at church." I also made a mental note not to accept initial impressions but to try the various positions enough times to get beyond the natural distractions of any "first try" phenomenon.

I had read that many of the early Christians believed the proper posture for prayer to be standing, with hands outstretched, and eyes lifted upward. Early church writers were willing to make allowances on the standing; anybody with foot or ankle trouble could sit. The sick could even lie down. But the hands outstretched and eyes raised upward were not very negotiable.

The early Christians' standing, hands out, eyes up posture was most likely a holdover from the traditional praying stance of Jews in the temple. Jesus' story about the Pharisee and the publican praying in the temple depicts the Pharisee doing everything according to the posture regulations of his time. He assumed the correct posture. But, Jesus tells us, "The Pharisee stood and prayed thus to himself" (Luke 18:11 NIV). Whether the preposition is translated "to himself," "with himself," or "about himself," it is obvious that the Pharisee had the right posture but the wrong prayer. His eloquent words were going nowhere except back into his own ears. The tax collector, on the other hand, broke the accepted practices for prayer posture. He was too ashamed to lift his eyes to heaven. His hands were not outstretched for they were too busy beating on his chest. And yet, Jesus said that the tax collector "went down to his house justified."

Posture lesson number one: certain physical postures may help enhance an attitude of worship but they cannot guarantee it. The posture of the heart is far more important in determining the success of our efforts to communicate with the Father. I recall with new appreciation the words of one prayer leader who used to say to the congregation, "Now, let us bow our heads and our hearts as we pray to God..."

I tried the standing, hands raised, eyes up posture. I tried it several times. The result was exactly what I had anticipated it would be. An eyes open praying position is just not going to work for me. When I tried it indoors, all I could think was, "That ceiling really needs painting." If I tried it outdoors, my mind drifted off into "Kinda cloudy today. Wonder if it's going to rain?" It is almost impossible for me to look at things and not see them. And if I see them, my mind is going to think about them and distracted thoughts are sure to follow.

Kneeling, with bowed head is another familiar posture to anyone who has read many Bible stories. Kneeling was a normal physical response back in the days when kings ruled and were always ready to fight for their authority. By kneeling before someone and lowering your gaze, you gave a clear sign that you were not contesting his or her authority. You were agreeing to be subservient. The appropriateness of kneeling continued even into modern centuries as long as kings and queens ruled.

Today, of course, the few royals who remain seem intent on demonstrating that they are no different from the rest of us. Furthermore, kneeling before another person is rarely a part of modern corporate or social etiquette. Some people feel that the physical act of kneeling still inspires the mind to adopt a spirit of adoration and worship. But in our democracy-dominated society, I almost never see anyone kneel in adoration outside of religious services.

Suppose, for example, that you are walking through an airport and you happen to see a famous celebrity whose achievements you have long held in high regard. You have an opportunity to meet that person. You may be fearful. You may be nervous. You may be tongue-tied. But it seems highly unlikely that you will step forward and kneel before the famous personality. The more typical response in our democratic times would be to reach out humbly, hoping for the chance to shake that person's hand and to speak a few words of admiration to him or her. Kneeling, like clerical collars and stained-glass windows, seems to require that a person be church-trained before it automatically signifies worship, submission, and adoration.

I tried the kneeling, head bowed posture. It was difficult for me to get past how my knees felt. If I were on a carpeted floor, they coped a little better than if I were on a non-carpeted floor. I was also conscious of my thigh muscles making adjustments to the unaccustomed balancing of knee standing. Bottom line on kneeling for me was that I could get used to it but did not feel a bit more "bowed" before God than I did sitting. The bowing of prayer seemed for me to be a thing that happened more in my attitude than in my posture.

While I was on my knees, I tried putting my head down to the floor. This is a prayer posture that has always impressed me when I have seen films of the Muslim faithful praying: changing alternately from kneeling to kneeling with head to the ground. My main distraction in this position was the fact that the blood kept running to my head. Maybe that's good. For me it was just a distraction.

I also tried what had always sounded to me like the most humble position of all: prostrate, face-to-the-ground. It is the position described for Jesus' prayer in Gethsemane in Matthew 26:36, though I cannot say whether Jesus was consciously adopting a certain position of prayer or simply falling face forward from total exhaustion and exasperation. At any rate, my prostrate, face-to-the-ground attempts all ended in puzzling thoughts about exactly how to do it. Should I turn my face to one side or the other, or do I lie with my nose mashed straight against the floor? Where do I put my hands? Above my head, out to the sides... where? Once again, I found that too much attention to the details of posture eliminated my mind's ability to summon up the attitudes of contrition and humility that the position was supposed to facilitate.

My experiments with positions of prayer did convince me of one thing. The most helpful prayer position for me is any position that doesn't make me aware of my position. Whether I am standing, sitting, lounging, or lying down, the fewer unusual things I do with my hands and arms, the less distracted I will be. Closed eyes are definitely important for me in minimizing distractions and focusing my mind on God.

I have heard of some people who like to pray as they walk. For me, that's not going to work. When I walk, I look. When I look, my mind is too busy to be directed at something I am looking at. "Eyes closed" is a definite help in my prayers except for those times when I am so concerned about something that my mind is focused on it more than on things I am looking at.

I am more and more impressed that for me the key to successful praying is doing whatever most helps my mind escape this earthly realm and focus its communication into the heavenly realm. My assumptions about where God is located are probably far less directional than the concepts of ancient people who benefited from kneeling or bowing because they thought of God as being spatially above, high above the clouds, or even beyond the stars.

I have no idea where God is located but I think of him as being in a different dimension rather than in a different location. Therefore, the more I can assume positions that make my body a non-factor, the more helpful it is to me. As mentioned in an earlier chapter, I often enjoy lying flat on my back, as physically relaxed as I can get, while my mind does the bowing and kneeling required for it to approach God appropriately.

Two stories on position in prayer are worth sharing, not just because they are humorous, but because they help drive home the idea that effective prayer is more a matter of the heart than of the position of the body. I remember hearing one elderly gentleman relate years ago that the most fervent prayer he remembered praying occurred while he was running as fast as his legs could carry him! The other line has to do with the man — either real or fictitious — who slipped and fell head first into a well. He later claimed that the "prayingest prayer" he ever said was when he was "standing on his head!"

In many of our prayers, we have a need to adopt a non-praying look. If we are to obey Jesus' instructions to "pray to our heavenly Father in secret," there will be some times when we want to pray without drawing the attention of those around us. I sat at a library table the other morning with a number of other people who were using the library. Resting my head on my hands above a book, I closed my eyes and allowed my mind to leave the scene and talk with God. If any one had asked, I would have been happy to tell them that I was praying. Otherwise, it seemed more appropriate not to blow the Pharisees' prayer trumpet in the library.

> *This body, Father, is so much in the way when I try to concentrate on you. I really like my body... Your design is wonderful and testifies to your divinity. But I am so attached to it that its aches and pains and positions get in the way of my communication with you. Help me to grow and mature, Father, to lessen the hold that my physical body has over my spiritual self. Get me ready for the brand new body you have promised. I can't wait to put it on, Lord.*
> *— Charlie.*

Chapter 17
Public Prayers
and Public Pray-ers

Many things that I think I understand about prayer simply go out the window when the subject changes from "a conversation between God and me" to "a conversation between God and me with other people listening." While I am confident that public prayers serve an important purpose, it still bothers me that they are, by nature, so different from private prayers. A public prayer is really a different animal altogether. In one sense, it is more like a sermon that somebody gets to preach without having to look the audience in the eye. When I lead the public prayer, I can say things to God about you that I might not have the guts to say to your face.

Of course, public prayers aren't the only times when we preach in our prayers. I think most of us preach to ourselves through our private prayers. I know I preach to myself whenever I put my inner thoughts into words that come out of my mouth and go right back into my ears. Some psychologists say that's all that really happens in prayer: that I get things out of my mind and onto the conscious level where I can do something about them. While I cannot agree that that is all that happens, I do think it is one of the great values of public or private prayer. As I articulate to God what is in my mind, I am also preaching to myself — exploring, convicting, challenging, and motivating.

Public prayer is hard to do well. The task of choosing a single set of words that can capture the concerns and yearnings of a whole group of people is a familiar one around churches. In some situations, I think that the traditional practice of asking one person to lead in prayer can do as much harm as good. Instead of singling out one person to demonstrate his or her ignorance or eloquence, we might more effectively accomplish the business of talking to God if we simply declared a time of prayer and let each person communicate (or nap) individually. At least, after a prayer like that, I would know whether I had personally prayed or not. When a prayer leader is up front intoning religious phrases as my mind wanders it is very easy for me to trick myself into thinking, as the final "amen" is pronounced, that I have actually participated in the prayer.

The traditional head-bowed-eyes-closed posture for congregational prayer can be a problem too. As one college student confided to me, "On Sunday morning after I have been up late on Saturday night, I make it okay until time for the first prayer. I'm fine through the announcements and scripture readings and the first few songs. But, when we bow our heads and close our eyes for the prayer, it's all over for me. I am asleep before the second sentence."

It is a tough assignment for any individual to stand up and choose a set of words that will satisfactorily represent the combined thinking of any diverse group of people, whether it be at the PTA or a civic club meeting. But if we add to the challenge the fact that church audiences have listened to the same list of prayer concerns year after year, the task of the prayer leader becomes particularly daunting. It's easy for the public prayer leader to be trapped between a desire to say those same old things in some creative new way and the ever-present temptation to stick to familiar phrasing and terminology so as not to jerk a worshipping audience out of its prayer comfort zone.

To realize how programmed we are as listeners to public prayers, think about the times you might have heard someone comment after services, "Well, I knew we were in for an extra long prayer when I saw Brother Jones step to the microphone." The concept of an "extra long prayer" results from the fact that the mental clocks of most regular church goers are preset for how long a prayer ought to run. We also know by heart the sequence of topics that are likely to be covered and if the prayer leader happens to wax eloquent and spend longer than usual on one of the topics at the first of the prayer, we may take a deep breath as if to settle in for a prayer marathon.

The leading of a public prayer also carries with it the added dimension of stage fright. Who among us is spiritually and psychologically secure enough to carry on a conversation with God without picturing our listeners with red grading pencils poised to mark each mispronunciation, grammatical error, and theological flub? In my opinion, one of the valid ways to measure the Christian maturity of a congregation of worshippers is the amount of stage fright that accompanies the assignment of leading a public prayer. The less stage fright, the greater the love and understanding among the members of that church family. If my relationship to

God and to my fellow Christians is open, honest, and sincere, then mistakes, corrections, or restatements in my prayer can be as normal and inconsequential as they are in my regular conversation.

For all the difficulties of public prayer, it must be noted that there is something wonderful happening when Christians pray together. For me to hear you intercede with God on my behalf produces a degree of encouragement that can hardly be equaled. I may know that you are concerned for me, but the moment I hear you articulate that concern in your own personal conversational style to our mutual Father I gain a level of love and appreciation for you that could not previously have existed.

We have a number of examples of Jesus praying publicly for the purpose of communicating important understandings to his followers. When he spoke the prayer that has come to be known as the "The Lord's Prayer," it was to teach a lesson on prayer. The entire seventeenth chapter of John's gospel is a prayer that Jesus prayed in his disciples' hearing on the night he was arrested. Those disciples needed to hear that prayer because many centuries later, you and I needed to hear the important principles of love and unity that Jesus articulated in his words to God. And perhaps the most interesting example of Jesus' teaching through public prayer occurred when he was about to raise Lazarus from the dead. In John 11:41-42, he said to God, "Father, I thank you that you have heard me. I knew that you always hear me, but I said this for the benefit of the people standing here, that they may believe that you sent me."

There are several characteristics that let me know

that a public prayer is about to rub me the wrong way — that I am going to have a hard time saying "amen" when it's over. If, for example, the prayer leader shifts into a different voice as the prayer begins, I start worrying that we are in for a prayer performance rather than a lay-it-on-the-line conversation with the Father. How must God feel when we lower our voices an octave and adopt an unnatural seriousness whenever we start talking to him? If I am a person who makes word-plays and jokes in my normal conversation, why wouldn't I talk to God the same way? Why should God have to put up with sad voices and sour expressions when we talk to him? Surely God has a sense of humor. Jesus' teaching was filled with funny lines and suggestions. I remember as a boy hearing someone joke, "We know God has a sense of humor because of all the funny-looking people he made."

Another red flag for me is the public prayer that sounds like a quilt of clichés stitched together with ancient terminology. I have no problem if a person uses "thees" and "thous" in prayer if they normally talk that way in every day life. But if thou adopteth an out-pouring of King James language only whensoever thou wouldest fain express thine adoration and show forth the fire that burneth in thine heart as the chosen messenger of thy brethren's sacrifice of prayer... I ain't buying it. Talk to God like you talk to me or I'm going to think you are putting both of us on.

Another thing. Even though characters in the Bible did it, I think it is humorous when we humans quote scripture to God in our prayers. I suppose it is reasonable that if we have become so familiar with the scriptural wording of some idea, we might use that same set of words when talking to the Father. But there have been a few times that I have sat in audiences and listened to my brothers quote scripture to God as if to argue him into submission on the requests at hand — like a child trapping a parent with the parent's own words. At the very least, we could pass up the tendency to remind God of the exact locations of the verses. Perhaps you have heard a well-meaning prayer leader say, "And we trust that you will grant our request, Father, because as you told us in Matthew chapter seven and verse eight, 'everyone who asks receives; and he who seeks finds.'"

Having now pointed out and ridiculed a few of our more common prayer habits, I want to back up and re-emphasize my opinion that you really can't pray wrong unless you are attempting to be dishonest with God. I am confident that God can hear us through our prayer clichés, in spite of our sanctimonious tones, and without being irritated by our quotes (and occasional misapplications) of scripture. What we have to realize is that as public prayer leaders, we have a special challenge to keep our own personalities out of the way. Our job is to facilitate the corporate prayer experience, not to perform it single-handedly.

Realizing this challenge, we have to choose our words and approaches in ways that will not distract — that will not get in the way of — the listening participants in the group prayer. In some of the most satisfying public prayers I remember leading, I took the term "prayer leader" quite literally and instead of doing all the talking about everything, I simply suggested a topic for which we all needed to pray and then kept quiet for a minute or two while each person in the audience spoke silently with God about that topic. After that moment of congregational silent prayer on a specific topic, I would suggest another topic that we all needed to address and shut up while the congregation prayed about it.

Many churches have retreated to pre-written prayers and prayer books as ways of avoiding the human oversights and failings that naturally creep into spontaneous public prayers. I think written prayers can be valuable, especially if they are written by the person who is going to deliver them. But I cannot escape my suspicion of a prayer originally articulated by a third-century Christian that is about to be read by a person living in the twenty-first century. There are probably times when it works well and can be very inspirational, but from my perspective, God would rather hear from me in spite of my flubs than to hear my third-century Christian brother's sentiments bubbling out of my mouth.

Just as no approach to our daily conversation is perfect for every situation, no style of prayer is right for every day. We adapt our ways of addressing each other according to the weather and how we are feeling at the time. Surely God would appreciate the same honest adaptations. Years ago, someone told me to beware of people whose personalities never changed from day to day, because they are playing a role. The same is probably true with the faces we turn to our heavenly Father in prayer. If we always sound happy or solemn or any certain way in our prayers, we are probably playing a role instead of laying it on the line with God — the God who already knows us through and through before we ever open our mouths.

Father,

When I stand up to lead a public prayer, please help me to forget myself and commit myself to being the spokesperson for the assembled group. Give me an extra measure of your Holy Spirit to stomp my ego, suppress my pride, and stop me from caring what anybody is thinking of me or my prayer-leading ability. Make me simply a channel of communication between you and your people — a channel that generates glory for you and for your Son. I love you.

— Charlie.

Chapter 18
Can I Substitute
Prayer for Sweat?

One of the continuing debates among religious people has to do with whether we please God by our faith or by our works. The debate is complicated even further by the fact that some of us claim to believe it all depends on God but then keep slipping back into our human inclination to want to do everything for ourselves. We talk faith... but live by works. Somehow, it never seems to occur to our human minds that in God's realm, every answer may not have to be either-or. Neither does everything about God have to occur in an earthly one-two-three sequence. I often wonder if God made us the way we are just for his entertainment... just to watch the hilarious knots we would tie our theologies into while trying to break the code that God is God and not just another human being we can force into our limited earthbound concepts and understandings.

The faith and works debate also extends to our confusions about prayer. There is a wide diversity of opinion as to whether God will actually answer prayer requests with work-saving miracles for us or whether we should, as the old saying goes, "Pray like it all depends on God and then work like it all depends on us." After all, Jesus himself repeatedly promised miraculous mountain moving capabilities to those who prayed with adequate faith. On the other hand, those of us who have actually tried moving a mountain by prayer have encountered results deprivation that could only be explained by admitting that we must not yet have reached a mountain-moving level of spiritual confidence.

Two familiar anecdotes represent these two views of prayer. The pray-but-sweat contingent is represented by the oft-quoted prayer of a grizzled old mountain man who was reported to have said, "Lord, I ain't asking for the faith that would move yonder mountain. I know how to move that mountain with dynamite. What I really need, Lord, is enough faith to move me." On the other hand, the expect-a-miracle crowd is fond of the story about the farmers who called a prayer meeting to pray for rain in the middle of an extended drought. They all showed up at the little church building but only one of them had enough faith to bring his umbrella!

We can also enlist scriptural support on either side of this discussion. Remember how God provided the daily manna for his Old Testament people to eat while they were wandering in the wilderness? It was free daily bread but they were still required to go out every morning and expend the energy required to pick it up. Jesus himself, in referring to all the multitudes who were being drawn to him by God, indicated in Matthew 9:38 that his followers should "Ask the Lord of the harvest, therefore, to send out workers into his harvest field." God was willing to initiate those miracles, but required some human participation to complete the jobs. On the other side of the topic, we read statements from James that shame the early Christians for not turning their needs completely over to God in confident prayer. In 4:2-3, James minces no words with his readers: "You do not have, because you do not ask God. When you ask, you do not receive, because you ask with wrong motives, that you may spend what you get on your pleasures."

I don't know many students who confidently expect God to give them a perfect score on a test they haven't studied for, though such prayer requests have definitely been dispatched as test papers were being handed out. Such ability would clearly constitute human wielding of miraculous power... and we humans are uncomfortable with miraculous powers. Though we are entertained by the likes of Houdini and Superman, we know deep down that miraculous powers would be unsatisfying even if we possessed them. Would you really want superhuman control of this world's events? Would you be able to wisely administer the crop from a money tree that sprouted in your back yard? Or might your uninformed and emotion-based decisions turn your superhuman powers toward helping some of the wrong people and penalizing some of the right people? Would the money tree in your back yard result in good things for the world, or in the total destabilization of the world monetary system?

I read recently of a situation where the answering of prayers took a curious turn. I don't know if it is a true story or one made up by someone who wanted to point out the humorous possibilities of supernatural powers in human hands. The story was set in a small village that had two churches and one whiskey distillery. The members of the two churches complained that the distillery gave the community a bad image. And, to make matters worse, the owner of the distillery was an outspoken atheist. Finally, the two churches scheduled a joint prayer meeting to ask God to intervene. As they prayed, a terrible electrical storm raged. Lightning struck the distillery and it burned to the ground. Fire insurance adjusters promptly notified the distiller that they would not pay for damages since acts of God were excluded from his policy. The distiller decided to sue the two churches, claiming that they had conspired with God to destroy his building. The church folks denied that they had anything to do with the cause of the fire. The judge expressed his amazement that the plaintiff, an atheist, was professing his belief in the power of prayer, while the defendants, all faithful church members, were denying that very same power.

The question is, does God give plain, everyday humans like you and me supernatural powers through prayer? Or does he reserve the distribution of heavenly intervention for himself? How true is the familiar church claim that "Prayer moves the hand that moves the world"? Some religious people are enthusiastic and adamant that they can and do personally distribute God's supernatural favors in the world. They point to their powers of physical healing and event alteration as proof that God endorses their work. Other religious people maintain that "the righteous shall live by faith" and that they know it is better to leave the application of supernatural powers up to a supernatural God.

Obviously, this little book is not going to answer such a long-standing question. The truth may be that both options are equally true and that God allows different answers to work for his children who have different needs. But one observation does seem to me to be undeniable: Given the power of word-of-mouth advertising and the natural human tendency to tell others about a good thing, any movement that actually possessed the on-call ability to heal the sick, raise the dead, and take away sadness would find the world beating down its doors and begging for membership. I do not see this unbiased endorsement of Christianity by the people of our world.

So, does God deputize us as prayer dispensers of supernatural powers or does he keep that power completely to himself? A young friend told me a personal experience that may actually prove both sides of the dilemma. "I have two friends at school that I've been wanting to share Christ with," my young friend said. "So, yesterday I asked God to open the door so they could receive the gospel. As I prayed, I was assuming that God would take over the job and use someone else to share with them. I really didn't feel confident about explaining it myself. But, as I was talking to them today, the door opened and I was able to share the gospel with them. I was honestly surprised when the door opened. God led them to ask questions that I could answer."

Jesus clearly spent a lot of his time dispensing his miraculous powers. Some scholars are quick to remind us that he did not heal every sick person in Palestine because his main reason for his miracles was to attract crowds and give credibility to his message. And yet, it is obvious that there were times when Jesus wanted to rest, had no desire to draw an audience, and yet surrendered his energy and time alone to heal the sick, simply because he had compassion on them.

Jesus not only did miracles himself, he deputized his followers to do the same. As his modern followers, most church members I know are a bit uneasy about the degree to which we can expect to actually request and receive miracles. We are totally turned off by side-show preachers who make healing an end in itself, but we are equally suspicious of the established church's tendency to make regular announcements, asking every member to offer up generic and non-specific prayers for "those who are sick of this congregation."

We pray for miracles, all the time wondering if God is still working that way. We may explain our lack of anticipation by saying that sometimes our prayers must be coupled with the skills of the doctors or modern medical technology. Or we explain that, in our times, God chooses to perform miracles on a more gradual time schedule than He did back in Bible times when lame men came leaping from their pallets the instant Jesus or his disciples said the word. But occasionally, we pray and instant miracles result. How do we explain that? Does it mean that instant miracles are out there just waiting for our requests? Was it a coincidence? Or could it be that God doles out his instant miracles according to some rule we don't understand?

Do you find it curious that we are ready and eager to pray for some types of miracles but would never even consider praying for other types of miracles? We will pour out our heart-felt concern for people who are starving in a famine and ask God to "help" them, but we would never presume to request a miraculous delivery of food as Jesus did. We will pray for a person's cancer to be miraculously healed but once that cancer has required a leg to be amputated, we would hardly think of praying for a healthy new leg to miraculously replace it. The weather and our physical health remain safe and open topics for prayer, but we almost never pray that evil people might be miraculously turned into good people. I have heard many a prayer leader ask God to "give us all a home in heaven" but I almost never heard one add the words "right now." Are we simply praying for the safe things: the ones that won't be too hard to explain if they happen? Are we carrying on honest, thoughtful communication with God or just playing around with the emperor's clothes again? Maybe our challenge is to pray for things that are so big that when they come to pass, there won't be any other explanation but that God did it.

A lot of what we tell each other in churches takes an emperor's-clothes approach to the kinds of results we can expect from prayer. It is especially easy for the children among us to hear our inspirational stories of miraculous outcomes and assume that such outcomes can be expected in every case. And since we rarely take the trouble to balance our descriptions by telling about all the prayers that do not bring inspiring results, the tragic result can be that when a young person does try prayer and miraculous results fail to come as automatically as promised, that person's faith in prayer can be dashed forever. I am afraid that the greatest encouragers of Christian skepticism about prayer are those of us who may have oversold the power of prayer in order to create a stirring ending for a sermon or a lesson.

Father,

Forgive me for my incessant desire to know all the answers. I'm so willful and proud that I just keep trying to control everything instead of letting you do it. Even when the only honest answer is that I don't know the answer, I still have a tendency to jump to some conclusion and then dig up a lot of verses to prove it. Help me, Father, to quit taking guesses and putting them out as truth. Give me peace in the knowledge that you are handling things and I don't have to know exactly how. I love you, Father. I trust you... even though I don't show it sometimes.
— Charlie.

Chapter 19
Persistent Prayer
or Browbeating God?

A Christian missionary in a foreign country is suddenly attacked by an unknown third-world parasite. As that missionary's physical body struggles to burn up the intruding parasite with fever, his spiritual body of Christian brothers and sisters begins simultaneously to fight the intruder by means of prayer. As the story of the missionary's illness and his doctors' inability to do anything about it spreads around the world at the speed of telephone, fax, and e-mail, more and more Christians join the prayer vigil. At all times of day and night, from all parts of the globe, Christians approach the throne of God with sincere requests for their fellow Christian — a man whom most of them have never met — to be returned to his former good health.

Soon, the good news arrives. To the amazement of the medical experts, the missionary's illness has been reversed! He is responding to treatment, growing stronger day by day, and attributing his cure to the world-wide army of people who have crowded the throne room of God with pleas for healing. What are we to conclude from such an experience? Does this mean that God can be intimidated into doing it our way if enough of us pound on his door and keep repeating our prayer petitions? Can we actually nag God into doing things our way? Is God like those human legislators who can be swayed on an issue if voters flood their offices with letters, telegrams, and telephone calls? Where would we have ever gotten such an impression about God?

Jesus himself planted this concept in our minds. On more than one occasion, Jesus told stories that encouraged us to stay on the line with God: to tell him over and over what we want. To me, one of Jesus' most humorous role-play parables was the one where he acted out the parts of the widow and the judge. In the first eight verses of Luke, chapter eighteen, Jesus tells about a poor widow who was simply not going to leave her local judge alone until he ruled in her favor. Picture Jesus acting out the story for the crowd, doing the voices of the widow and of the judge. The judge is in his court and the widow insists, "Grant me justice against my adversary." The judge starts home at the end of the day and is followed by a widow who keeps chanting, "Grant me justice against my adversary." He is awakened at daybreak by a widow under his window whispering, "Grant me justice against my adversary." As he eats his breakfast, the judge listens to a rhythmic repetition from outside his door: "Grant me justice against my adversary." Day after day... "Grant me justice against my adversary."

With each repetition, Jesus' audience is laughing a little harder and getting the message a little clearer. Finally, Jesus shifts abruptly to do the lines of the judge. "All right!" he storms. "Even though I don't fear God or care about men, yet because this widow keeps bothering me, I will see that she gets justice, so that she won't eventually wear me out with her coming!" To my ears, Jesus is giving the judge in his little drama the humorously unlikely lines, "Look, folks. I know I'm the appointed bad guy in this play — the low-down rat with no scruples or integrity — but even a villain knows when he's had enough. I am giving this woman whatever she wants before she drives me nuts! Until I get this woman off my back, I'll never have a moment's peace. Even a bad guy has his limits, you know."

Jesus gives us no clue as to whether the widow's cause was right or wrong. His point is that she was persistent. The simple lesson of Jesus' story is that if an unrighteous judge is going to be influenced by repetitious requests, imagine how much more a loving heavenly father is likely to listen to our oft-repeated prayers.

Persistence is a life concept we understand. We love those stories of the person who wants something so strongly that he or she will simply not give up. We cheer as the determined person pushes, pulls, claws, and scratches all the way to eventual success. We like to hear inspirational speakers tell us that "big shots are just little shots who kept on shooting," that by tenacity we can "climb every mountain," and that, in the words of Winston Churchill, we should "never, never, never give up."

Yet, the same Jesus who told us to keep on asking also discouraged us from being like the scribes and Pharisees "who think they will be heard because of their many words" (Matthew 6:7 NIV). Why would Jesus encourage us to keep on asking, yet warn us not to put our dependence in the fact that we keep on asking?

In our admiration of Christian persistence, there

lurks a danger that we might actually enter into a sort of competition with God, an unintentional struggle to see who is in control. It is one thing for us to want something so strongly that we can think of nothing else — that we cannot stop expressing our desires about it to God in prayer. But it is something entirely different when we adopt an attitude of competition with God. Think of the times you have heard calls for everyone to pray earnestly for something. Is the implication that so many of us will be praying for this need that we will tie up all God's communication lines, surround heaven like strikers with placards, overwhelm God with our echoing demands, and eventually force him to see things our way? And if we were able to mobilize our praying forces in such a way that we could dependably make God give in to our wishes, who would then be God — he or we?

There is an ever-present danger when we start trying to talk God into things. My ways are not his ways. My motives are not his motives. And yet, I have caught myself trying to coax God to take action. "Just think about it, God," I whisper in my most convincing voice. "If you were to grant this prayer that so many people in our church are praying, to grant it in a way that they would know it was a direct answer to their prayers, just think of how much more they would believe in you. Just think of the way their faith in you would increase and grow."

Once again, I am putting myself in competition with God. I am trying to be the power behind the throne, the royal counselor who whispers into the king's ear and controls the royal decree. God is not an ignorant human king who needs human handlers to suggest wise actions. God is God. He knows what he is doing and fortunately is willing to love me in spite of my childish efforts to sway his actions. He knows, for example, that my human desire for highly visible connections between what I ask and what He gives is not going to move me toward greater faith but toward less faith and more confidence in what I see. If I can predictably see the results of my prayers, I have moved out of the realm of faith and into the realm of sight. The Bible is emphatic that "the righteous shall live by faith" (Habakkuk 2:4, Romans 1:17, Galatians 3:11, and Hebrews 10:38). According to Hebrews 11:1, "faith is being sure of what we hope for and certain of what we do not see." But if my religion is founded on the stories I can tell you about specific requests that I convinced God to grant, my confidence has shifted from things not seen to things seen.

The Bible reveals to us that there are supernatural powers that are not God. If I were the evil one and my purpose was to divert people from God, I think I would spend a lot of time whispering into the ears of praying people... telling them that if they do their praying by some correct formula they will soon have God at their command. I would take every opportunity to deliver to them unwise things they prayed to God for. I would give them confidence in their own prayer power to the extent that they would eventually consider it a vehicle for getting what they want instead of an opportunity to commune and communicate with creation's ultimate power.

So, persistence in prayer is one more aspect of the life of faith in which I am faced with the necessity of maintaining balance. I am to persist in prayer. Yet, I am never to assume that my persistence is the secret of forcing God to obey me. My repetitious prayers should result from my sincere desire for the object of my prayers, not from the assumption that God has set some magic number of requests and when I have finally asked that many times, he will grant my request.

Most important of all, I must utter each and every prayer request in full understanding of my relationship with God. He is God; I am not. He is the one who knows what is best for me. I have proven time and again that I do not know what is best for me. Every word that I utter to him must be wrapped in the confident understanding that no matter what I am wishing for, it will be best if God's will is done.

> God,
>
> I keep realizing that most of what I go through in my life is to help me get straight the one most important fact: that you are God and I am not. When I am focused on that truth, things seem to work for me, Father. When I forget that truth and start trying to manipulate you, the wheels come off my wagon. Bless me, Father, with unbroken awareness of your divinity and my dependence. Let me see my prayers as times of blessed communication with you... not times when I unload my list of wishes on you. Thank you for loving me even when I forget.
> — Charlie.

Chapter 20
So, It All Comes
Down To...

This book sat at a complete standstill, right here at the beginning of this chapter, for over a year. Up to this point, it flowed along rather efficiently and on schedule. But a funny thing happened on the way to the last chapter of the book. Writing a book about prayer made me start praying more frequently and more honestly. In a way that I never had, I laid things on the line with God. It seemed only fair that, if I were going to encourage you to be absolutely honest with God, I should be doing the same thing myself. So, I told God that whatever he had in mind for my life, I was ready to trust him to do it. He took me at my word. And he has kept me so busy living my prayers during the past year that there's been no time to finish a book about prayer.

The more I prayed, the less comfortable I was spending most of my time and energy earning a living and then tossing God my left-over time by teaching an occasional Bible class. So, I opened my big mouth and told God that I wanted to either get in or get out of this discipleship thing. It was clear to me that life is too short to play church. I told God that I was ready to put his kingdom absolutely first in my life, that I was going to take him at his word and believe his promise that all the other necessities would be supplied. I promised him that I would stop trying to make my own plans and would make every effort to relinquish control of my highly self-controlled life. I apprehensively read and re-read the assurances of Jesus that food, clothing, and shelter would be supplied if I would just put God first. And I prayed, "Lord, I'm going to give it a shot. I'm going to put your people first. I'm going to teach... and counsel... and pray... and serve them as you send them to me. I'll keep earning a living as I have time but I'm going to trust you to set the schedule and provide the income that Kay and I need."

No sooner did I make that promise than the floodgates of God's opportunities opened. Opportunities to serve in the name of Jesus began to flow. The church family of which we had been a part for twenty-five years asked me to serve as one of its spiritual leaders. That request had been made several times in previous years, but I had always declined knowing my tendency to do things wide open or not at all — and knowing that working as hard as I could year after year, we had only barely been able to keep our family bills paid. This time, I accepted. "Okay, God," I prayed. "Here I am... climbing out toward the end of this limb. You're on, God. Don't let me down."

I became one of eleven shepherds guiding the spiritual growth of a congregation of about 600 people. The hours spent in prayer with my fellow shepherds were times of growth, dedication, and hard spiritual work. Our common dedication to "getting ourselves out of the way" so that God could take the leadership of our flock was the beginning of a wonderful time of spiritual renewal. The love flowed. Our congregation grew in

Jesus. Jesus grew in us. Many members of our church family had clearly been working up to the same kind of "get in or get out" commitment. We began to experience the highest level of sustained joy and dedication I had ever known in fifty years of doing church. We certainly did not create a heaven on earth. The devil was alive and well and taking prisoners on a regular basis. But the common desperation of forgiven sinners doing their best to keep each other in the lifeboat created a wonderful atmosphere of honesty and sincerity, a willingness to lay ourselves on the line with God.

And our family income? The long-term results are yet to be seen. At this point, my income is about half what it has been in previous years, but my joy in life is at least twice what it has ever been. God has already come through with some impressive surprises: checks for writing assignments I never expected to get paid for, an out-of-the-blue invitation to do some writing for a prestigious company I had been trying to crack for fifteen years, and several writing jobs that I somehow finished in half the time they used to take. Maybe God is planning to continue supporting us that way. Or maybe Kay and I just need to learn to live on half as much as we used to live on. Either way, we like our life a whole lot better with God doing the decision making. We've always lived pretty much hand to mouth. Now it's just a lot clearer to us that it's God's hand and our mouths.

I could have been more careful with prayer. I could have held God at arm's length with the continued use of well-worn phrases in thoughtless prayers. But the more I learned about Jesus and his way in our world, the more I could see that he had complete mastery of life situations that were regularly mastering me. I wanted to be best friends with that kind of power. I wanted to be in Jesus as I could tell he was in God. I started talking honestly with God about it. He, of course, had been listening all the time, just waiting for me to catch on. He heard my prayers. He changed my life.

As a teenager, I had been born again into Jesus and buried with him in baptism. God forgave my sins and gave me the gift of his own Spirit. Through many years, he faithfully supported my maturing in Christ and rewarded each effort I made to serve him. Now, once again, he was ready to honor my new resolve with a flood of growth opportunities. The tension between faith and sight has always been a way of life for God's people, yet God remains ready to reward each feeble attempt to live by faith. I laid it on the line with God. He took me at my word. He has delivered on his promises.

So, it all comes down to the fact that prayer is the barometer of faith. As my prayer life goes, so goes my faith. In my relationship to God, faith is the whole ball game. If I hold God at arm's length when I pray, he will let me keep my distance. If I keep a tight grip on the reins of my life as I pray, God will listen lovingly without snatching away the reins. But... when I finally laid my life on the line with God in prayer, he realigned my life in the most wonderful way. Someone summarized my experience the other day when he said, "The main thing is making the main thing the main thing." How true! The main thing (for your life and mine) is making the main thing (in God's eyes) the main thing (that occupies our hearts and minds and energies).

Prayer can only be proven by praying. Faith only becomes faith after you take the first baby steps of believing. It is part of the great mystery of life that we never succeed in anything until we summon up enough risk-taking desperation to give it a first try. Try praying. Say what you feel. If you can't pray to God in faith, pray to him in doubt and ask him what he can do about getting you some faith. If God is there listening, he can certainly handle your honest doubt and he has the power to take over and build on your feeble beginning. If God is not there, it won't matter what you say. In fact, nothing else will really matter, given a hundred years or so. Since you are on thin ice anyway, you might as well dance. If there is no God, then talking to your ceiling is no crazier than any other way you might spend your time. If there is a God, there is nothing more important for you than establishing contact and laying your guts on the line with him.

> *Dear Father,*
>
> *Thank you for being there. Thank you for being the loving Father who leads me through daily learning, toward the attitudes and appreciations that will make eternal life with you so rewarding. I ask you to go with the words of this book into the mind and spirit of each reader. Make these words useful tools in your hands to bring us all more completely into you. Thank you for saving me through the sacrifice of your son, Jesus. It is in his name that I pray and live.*
> *— Charlie.*

Suggested Readings

à Kempis, Thomas, *The Imitation of Christ*, Translated by P.G. Zomberg, Dunstan Press, Rockland, Maine, 1984.

Buttrick, George A., *Prayer*, Abingdon Press, New York, 1942.

Chambers, Oswald, *My Utmost for His Highest*, Discovery House Publishers, Grand Rapids, MI, 1992.

Foster, Richard J., *Prayer, Finding the Heart's True Home*, Harper San Francisco, 1992.

Gallup, George, Jr, and Poloma, Margaret, *Varieties of Prayer: A Survey Report*, Trinity Press, Valley Forge, PA, 1991.

Girzone, Joseph F., *Never Alone*, Doubleday, New York, 1994.

Greeley, Andrew M., *Love Affair: A Prayer Journal*, Crossroad Publishing Company, New York, 1992.

Hulme, William E., *Celebrating God's Presence*, Augsburg Publishing House, Minneapolis, MN., 1988.

Ikerman, Ruth C., *Let Prayer Help You*, Christian Herald Books, Chappaqua, NY, 1980.

Marshall, Catherine, *Adventures in Prayer*, Chosen Books, Old Tappan, N.J., 1975.

McGarvey, J.W., *Sermons Delivered in Louisville,*

Kentucky, "Prayer: Its Efficacy," Standard Publishing Company, Cincinnati, OH, 1893.

Meneilly, Robert, *Pray As You Go*, Andrews and McMeel, Kansas City, MO, 1996.

Miller, Keith, *The Taste of New Wine*, Word Books, Waco, 1965.

Murray, Andrew, *The Prayer Life*, Whitaker House, Springdale, PA, 1981.

Paulsell, William O., *Rules for Prayer*, Paulist Press, New York/Mahwah, N.J. 1993.

Pennington, M. Basil, *Centering Prayer*, Doubleday & Company, Inc., Garden City, NY, 1980.

Peterson, Lorraine, *Please Give Me Another Chance, Lord*, Bethany House Publishers, Minneapolis, 1995.

Phillips, J.B., *Your God Is Too Small*, Macmillan, New York, 1960.

Price, Eugenia, *What Really Matters*, The Dial Press, New York, 1983.

Rinpoche, Sogyal, *The Tibetan Book of Living and Dying*, Harper San Francisco, 1992.

Sherrer, Quin, and Garlock, Ruthanne, *The Spiritual Warrior's Prayer Guide*, Servant Publications, Ann Arbor, Michigan, 1992.

Stedman, Ray C., *Jesus Teaches on Prayer*, A series of sermons preached at Peninsula Bible Church, Palo Alto, CA, 1964, www.pbc.org:80/dp/stedman/jprayer/

Thomas, Leslie G., *Let Us Pray!*

Discussion and Study Questions

1. **The Emperor's Clothes?**

   - One of the early statements in Chapter 1 suggests that "most folks think they understand prayer pretty well." Do you agree or disagree? Why?

   - What is your reaction to the statement that "as many as a fifth of people who claim to be atheists or agnostics pray with some regularity"?

   - Can you identify at all with the writer's description of faith that comes and goes, that is alternately strong and weak?

   - Do you feel that the writer was justified in comparing our attitudes about prayer to the story, "The Emperor's New Clothes"?

2. **Prayer? Nothing To It.**

   - How adequate is the child's definition that "prayer is when you're talking to God"? What important aspects of prayer do you think that simplistic statement leaves out?

   - Do you agree or disagree with the statement, "most of us can agree on what prayer is but that the real questions start with how prayer is done"? Can you give examples of some of the questions about how we should pray?

- What were the conditions under which your most meaningful and fulfilling prayers occurred?

- The chapter mentions several kinds of paraphernalia that people use in prayer. What is your opinion about the use of candles, beads, written notes, altars, or prayer wheels? Do they help or hurt?

- Have you had the experience described as discovering "that we have been praying without realizing it"? How is that possible?

- Why does prayer seem to work differently in the movies than it does in real life?

- Do you agree or disagree with the assertion that all people need God?

3.   **All I Really Want is Everything.**

- What percent of prayers would you guess are for the purpose of trying to get things from God?

- What answer would you give to the little girl who said, "I have been praying hard every night for God to give me a horse... but he doesn't do it."

- How small or inconsequential a thing do you think is appropriate to bother God about in prayer? Should we reserve our prayer requests for the really serious things?

- Paul said that God is able to do "immeasurably

more than all we ask or imagine..." What's the biggest answer to prayer that you have ever observed?

- How does Jesus' suggestion that his disciples would have to become childlike apply to prayer?

- Do you think that God invented selfishness? If so, why would he do such a thing?

4. What's the Deal Here, God?

- How do you usually explain it to yourself or others when God fails to come across with the goods or services you have requested in prayer?

- Do you think it was a real promise or just sermonizing when Jesus told the multitudes, "Ask and it shall be given to you..."? Is it true or not?

- How do you feel about the idea of grumbling at God when your prayers don't go as you had hoped or expected they would?

- Can you think of times that people you knew misunderstood or misapplied one of God's promises in prayer?

- Describe how your day might go — from the beginning of your day until bedtime — if God were to actually give you anything you asked for in prayer?

- Do you recall times when you begged your parents for things and could not understand why they continued to deny your requests? How did you see that situation differently after becoming a parent? Have there been ways that your understanding of God changed after you became a parent?

- How important is it to make the distinction between the things we want and the things we need?

- Can you think of times when you have been guilty of praying as if God were the "cosmic bellhop"?

- How might it cause you to live less by faith and more by sight if your prayers gave you human control of God's miraculous power?

5. **Plunk Your Magic Twanger, Froggy.**
- Would you agree or disagree with the statement, "God does magic when he answers our prayers"?

- Is your faith (or lack of it) connected in any way to some time when God either granted or refused to grant your prayer request? Describe the situation.

- How can you tell the difference between a prayer that God answers and a prayer that gets answered by luck or coincidence?

- How do you feel about the popular saying, "there are no coincidences"?

- Why should we expect God to answer everyone's prayers according to the same rules?

- How does it make you feel to hear the statement, "God is very often answering a completely different question from the one I am so focused on"? Do you feel better or worse knowing that?

6. Thou Shalt Not Pray!

- How believable is the story about Herrick Hargreaves? Would anyone in real life ever be so consciously dedicated to undermining the faith of believers?

- Can you see how Herrick Hargreaves might have gotten the idea that Christianity is "mankind's way of running away from problems instead of solving them"? How might you respond to this charge?

- How big a temptation would $65 a week be for you? Could the devil buy you off your faith for that amount? Would it make a difference if the amount were $65,000 a week?

- What examples can you think of where people traded their beliefs for a lot less than $65 a week? What non-monetary things can tempt us away from our God?

- If you were re-setting the story of Daniel in modern times, how would the story line go? Where would it take place? Who would be the bad guys? What would they do? How would the story go if the Daniel character were in your shoes?

- Does it bother you that God saved Daniel

from the lions and then, centuries later, let the lions in Rome gobble up faithful Christian martyrs? How can this be explained?

7.   **What If I Pray Wrong?**

- Where did you get your ideas about prayer? Would you have thought of prayer as a thing to do if people you knew had never mentioned it? Does each person have a natural understanding of what's right or wrong in prayer, or do we have to be taught those concepts as we grow up?

- Some people feel that using "thee" and "thou" in our prayer language shows proper respect for God. Others think there's no point in talking to God in one way and everyone else in another way. Which position is correct? Could both positions be correct? Explain.

- Do you find the analogy of the child talking to his father helpful in understanding prayer? How does your relationship with your own father effect the way you hear this analogy? Are there limitations to this analogy, ways that it falls short of representing God or his communication with us?

- Are you ever angry with God? How honestly are you able to pray when this is the case?

- Do you ever say spontaneous, single-thought prayers to God? What kinds of things most often cause you to do so?

- Do you ever catch yourself trying to lie to God? Why do you think we sometimes try to lie to God even when we know that he is fully aware of everything in our minds at all times?

8.   Even Asking for the Bad Stuff!

- Do you agree or disagree with the sentiment, "the older I get the more I pray, but the less likely I am to tell God exactly how I think he should respond"? Shouldn't we be getting wiser as we grow older?

- What is the meaning of the line, "some of God's greatest gifts are unanswered prayers"? Are there really any unanswered prayers?

- Have you ever been denied something that you prayed hard for, only to realize years later that you were fortunate not to receive it? Or have you ever prayed for something, received it, and realized years later that God could have done you a big favor by denying that request? Why would God ever grant requests for things that are not good for us?

- Where are you in the developmental transition from trying to control God to letting God control you? Can you say with real honesty, "not my will, Father, but yours be done"?

- How do you feel about asking God for things like unemployment, poverty, failure, drudgery, rejection, sickness, or death?

9.   **What We Have Here is a Failure to Communicate**

- Did you agree with the five parts suggested for any communication situation (sender, receiver, message, medium, and interference) or did you think of other factors that should be added into the formula?

- How can "silent togetherness become a pleasurable communication in itself"?

- Do you think it would help your prayers to listen more? How would you go about doing this? Do you believe God communicates with us when we pray? Why or why not?

- When you pray to God, what mental picture do you have in your mind? Are you picturing God as you are talking to him? What does your mental picture of God look like? How would your prayers change if you had a different picture?

- Why is it so important for Christians to know that God has promised in Romans 8:26 to send his own spirit to put into words those things we cannot express? Do you ever sense this activity of the Spirit taking place as you are praying?

- How do you respond to the idea, "words are our least effective method of communication... especially when we are talking to God"?

- What are some things you can do to better prepare yourself to pray?

10. **Remembering You Always in My Prayers**

- Have you tried using a written prayer list? Did it help or hinder? Do you feel that going down the list can hinder the heart-felt nature of prayers?

- How did it make you feel when the author moved his written prayer list from hand-written notes to a computer program? Too mechanical? Too impersonal? No difference?

- What are some of the times you have seen intercessory prayer result in significant changes in a situation? What percentage of your prayer time would you say is intercessory?

- What good does it do to pray for friends who are grieving the loss of a loved one? Since there's no bringing back the person they lost, what should you ask God to do for them? How long do you think grieving persons should be left on the prayer list?

- The Bible tells us about Jesus praying for long periods of time. Can you picture Jesus using a written prayer list to remind him of people or things he wanted to pray about, or do you think Jesus had super-human memory?

- Have you ever prayed for your enemies? Did it make a difference? What happened?

11. **The Ultimate E-Mail**

- Do you have a best time of day to pray? When is it? How do your prayers at that time differ from your prayers at other times of the day?

- The author describes his somewhat humorous attempts to pray in the early morning. What would you say was his main problem? What was the main thing getting in the way of a satisfying pre-dawn prayer rendezvous with God?

- How literally should we take Paul's instruction in 1 Thessalonians 5:17 to "pray without ceasing"? What changes would you make in your day if you decided to really pray without ceasing?

- Are you comfortable with the comparison of prayer to e-mail? Does it seem a little sacrilegious? How meaningful do you find the concept of "G-mail?"

- How do you like the Christian game-playing suggested in the chapter? How do you feel about picturing yourself as a secret agent maintaining continuous and secret radio contact with headquarters as you go about the activities of your daily schedule? Would it help you?

- In light of the ancient practice of having ritual sentence prayers for specific activities of the day, are there certain activities of your day that could really benefit from their own special sentence prayers?

- In our prayers to God, what's the difference between the "small talk" and the "major speeches"?

12. Might As Well Lay It On the Line

- Whom can you name in your circle of associates that is going to love you regardless of whether you do well or mess up? How important is this kind of love to you? Have you ever thanked them for such love?

- How did you feel about the picture of God sitting in a heavenly control room watching little video monitors that report the condition of each of our hearts? Did you get stuck trying to picture billions of little monitors? Did you find the visual image helpful or distracting? Why do we usually run into problems when we try to explain God in human terms?

- Why do you suppose is it so hard for us to remember that God looks at the heart instead of the outward appearance?

- How would you like "a day's pass to sin without it counting"?

- Do you agree with the statement, "It is only from the human perspective that sins can be ranked small, medium, and large"? Aren't some sins clearly a lot worse than other sins? What's the difference in socially acceptable sins and socially unacceptable sins?

- Do you think a person can be so honest with God that he or she is actually praying to God at the very moment he or she is disobeying God and sinning? How could we do such a thing? What difference might it make?

13. Shut Up and Listen!

- What do you think it reveals about us when we have more trouble listening than talking?

- How do you feel about the definition of true listening as "trying to see things the other person's way"? Is it good to listen sympathetically when you are discussing things with a person whose viewpoint is evil? What if we become too sympathetic and begin to really see it their way?

- Are we really praying to God when we are just being quiet, clearing our minds of all thoughts, and saying nothing? How can silence be prayer?

- How do you feel about riding in the car alone with the radio turned off, or sitting for long periods of time with nothing to read and no television playing? How long can you be happily alone with your own thoughts?

- What prepping techniques do you think are likely to work best for you — likely to help you be ready to be quiet and listen for God?

- How did the idea of meditating in your "one-button suit" strike you? Do you feel that God would be pleased or displeased if you approached him for prayer or meditation when you were absolutely naked?

14. Does God Speak Olde English?

- Picturing a God who is fluent in all the earth's 3,000 languages is difficult for us. What do you suppose this difficulty tells us about God and about our ways of understanding him?

- What is the meaning of the statement, "Prayer is a good barometer of faith"?

- Is the good news of Jesus Christ really as understandable to an illiterate person as it is to a learned one? What percentage of the Christians we read about in the book of Acts, do you suppose, could read and write?

- Which do you prefer in church: ritual or spontaneous prayers? Which do you think God prefers? What are the pros and cons of using the prayers penned by great Christians who lived long ago?

- What is it about religious people that makes it so hard for them to say, "I prefer this and you prefer that," and so easy for their opinions to push them into the sad corner of "I am right and you are wrong"?

15. Do I Get Extra Points for Praying on Mountaintops?

- How do you react to the statement "Almost everything any of us know we learned from movies or television"?

- Do you agree with the author's description of the Hollywood version of Jesus going up in the hills to pray? Do you assume that it was really that perfect for Jesus, or was his list of real-world trials and distractions just as numerous as ours? Would Jesus respond differently than you to a spider web that wrapped itself around his face as he walked up the mountain path?

- Is it easier to pray in beautiful scenic settings than in your normal everyday location? Why or why not?

- What have you found to be the best time and setting for you to pray?

16. Do Kneelers Get Preferential Treatment?

- One writer of the last century stated adamantly, "...it should be remembered, that while standing and kneeling are both marks of respect in the presence of a superior, sitting is not; and consequently, sitting in prayer betrays a want of reverence." (J.W. McGarvey, *The New Testament Commentary*, Vol. I—Matthew and Mark, 339.) Do you agree or disagree?

- Do you think posture in prayer is more a matter of culture, the times, personal preference, or God's requirement?

- What do you think is meant by the phrase "the posture of the heart"?

- What are your assumptions about where God is located? Do you think of him as being up in the sky, inside your heart or mind, in another dimension altogether, or some other concept? How does this concept affect your prayers?

17. **Public Prayers and Public Pray-ers.**

- Have you heard public prayers that demonstrated greater awareness of the audience listening than of God listening? What kinds of statements can reveal this misplaced emphasis?

- Why do you think it makes so much difference to speak our private prayer thoughts into audible words? Aren't those thoughts already in our minds?

- What are some of the characteristics of the public prayer situation that make it so difficult to do well? What things must the leader of a public prayer strive to overcome?

- Are there certain traditional words or phrases almost certain to be included if a prayer is to remain within the prayer comfort zone where you worship?

- What can be done to reduce the stage fright of persons who are unaccustomed to leading prayers in front of church audiences?

- Why do you think it helps Christians to hear other Christians pray for them?

- How would you feel about a person who made a joke or a pun in the middle of a public prayer? Would this be sacrilegious or show disrespect for the creator of heaven and earth?

- What are some things we might do as public prayer leaders to keep our own personalities out of the way of those we are trying to lead?

18. Can I Substitute Prayer for Sweat?

- Are we saved by our faith, by our works, or by both? Is this a question that is beyond complete human comprehension?

- How about the promises Jesus made to his disciples about moving mountains through prayer? Did Jesus really mean that real believers could actually move literal mountains around the surface of the earth, or was he just using a figure of speech?

- Look again at James 4:2-3. Is this passage making a literal promise about our ability to get things by just praying for them? Are there any limitations to what we might ask for? What do wrong motives have to do with the promise?

- What would you do with the crop from a money tree that sprouted in your back yard? Do you think God would be happy or sad if he were to trust you with absolute magical powers?

- How true is the familiar church claim, "Prayer moves the hand that moves the world"?

- Does the fact that people are not rushing to become Christians prove that Christian claims of the power of prayer are not really true? If prayer really changes things, why aren't more people lining up to pray?

- Do you think God still does instant miracles in our times? If he no longer works as he did in the Bible accounts, why do you suppose he changed?

- Have you prayed for God to change the normal course of events and seen that change take place? Have you prayed for God to change the normal course of events and seen no change occur? What do you suppose made the difference in the prayer that was "answered" and the prayer that wasn't?

19. Persistent Prayer or Browbeating God?

- Do you think God is more likely to grant a prayer request if a great number of his children are simultaneously begging for the same thing?

- Why should God be influenced by persistent, repeated prayers more than by a single request? Would this mean God is swayed by popular demand? If God can be manipulated by "prayer-a-thons," would that mean that he is not really in control at all, but under subjection to organized prayer initiatives?

- Why do you think Jesus would encourage us to keep on asking (as in his story of the widow and the unrighteous judge), yet tell us to put no dependence in the fact that we keep on asking (as in his warnings about the Pharisees who thought they would be heard "for their much speaking")?

- What possible interest could the evil one have

in seeing that our prayers are granted? Can you think of any way that the devil could turn an answered prayer to his advantage?

20. So, It All Comes Down To...

- What do you suspect might happen if you let God have complete control of your life? How might your daily routine and activities be different a year from now if you held nothing back from God's control?

- How do you think God would like it if you said you wanted to "either get in or get out of this discipleship thing"? Could you say it and mean it? Is half-hearted discipleship better than no discipleship at all?

- How does your life style match up with the concept of "living hand to mouth"? What difference might it make if you were more aware that it is God's hand and your mouth?

- Do you agree with the statement, "As my prayer life goes, so goes my faith"? If that is true, would the ever-present need to increase your faith become a simple matter of praying more? Which comes first: the faith or the prayer?

- How reasonable is the suggestion of praying to God whether you believe in him or not? Why would you waste time talking to a God that you did not even believe was there? If you reveal your honest doubts and God really is there, might he not get mad and punish you?